Praise for *THE NEW MARKETING MISSION*

"This book is a roadmap to the future of marketing. Ignore it at your peril, because your competition will surely jump on it."

> — *Bob Wehling, Former Global Marketing Officer,*
> *Procter & Gamble*

"*The New Marketing Mission* will do for marketing what *The Wealth of Nations* did for economics or *Origin of the Species* did for our view of evolution. It is a groundbreaking work that shatters our preconceived notions about marketing and a work that will frame our dialogs and debates about marketing for the next decade."

> — *Peter Sealey, Former Global Marketing Manager,*
> *The Coca-Cola Company*

"Pascal asked, 'Heart or Reason, which one to follow?' Is great marketing only inspiration and gut feeling? No—good measures, good tools and process can support inspired marketing, and build strong companies that win in the marketplace. *The New Marketing Mission* gives both Pascal and the CMO new food for thought."

> — *Elio Leoni-Sceti, Executive VP Category Development,*
> *Reckitt Benckiser*

"Through our involvement with the ANA, P&G has begun working with other thought leaders to help create a new marketing approach in these rapidly changing times. This provocative book captures many of the concepts in which we believe: (1) the mindset that "the Consumer is Boss"; (2) the focus on the marketing process for ensuring plans reflect vital consumer insights; (3) the use of technology to unleash creativity, innovation, and growth in marketing; and (4) the absolute necessity of measuring each component of the marketing demand creation mix."

> — *From the Foreword by Jim Stengel,*
> *Global Marketing Officer, Procter & Gamble,*
> *and Chairman, Association of National Advertisers*

The New Marketing Mission

How Process, Metrics, and Technology Can Unleash Growth

Hunter Hastings
Gordon Wade
Sat Duggal
with Jeff Saperstein

Association of National Advertisers
708 Third Avenue   •   New York, NY 10017-4270
www.ana.net

Project manager and editor: *Jeff Saperstein*
Production manager and designer: *Vanessa Moore*
Cover designer: *Jerry Votta, Chuti Prasertsith*
Copyeditor: *Lawrence Hargett*
Proofreader: *Teresa Horton*

© 2004 EMM Group, Inc.
P.O. Box 50767
Kalamazoo, MI 49005
Published by the Association of National Advertisers, Inc.

For information regarding ordering in bulk, please contact:
ANA, 708 Third Ave., New York, NY 10017-4270, *www.ana.net.*
EMM Group, Inc., P.O. Box 50767, Kalamazoo, MI 49005, *www.emmgroup.net.*

Printed in the United States of America
2nd Printing, February 2005

ISBN 1-56318-032-4

Contents

Chapter 2

What's New: End-to-End Content Multiplied by End-to-End Technology   19

Part II • Processes for Long-Term Brand Building and Planning   41

Chapter 3

Insights: The Heart of the Brand   43

Chapter 4

Domain Strategy: A Powerful Growth Stimulus for Brands in Every Industry   59

Chapter 5

Building Brand Equity: Brand Vision and Brand Challenge   77

Chapter 6

Long-Term Equity Plan: Brand Imperatives   95

PART III • Processes for Brand Implementation   113

Chapter 7

Building a Plan with an Integrated Marketing Strategy   115

Chapter 8

Functional Excellence   125

Chapter 13

What Should You Do on Monday Morning?   191

About the Authors

 Hunter Hastings is the father of enterprise marketing management. After a 25-year career in brand management and marketing consulting, he led the initiation of the EMM movement as CEO of Emmperative, a company dedicated to bringing process, metrics, and technology to marketing, funded by Procter & Gamble and Accenture. He continues this lifework as Managing Partner of EMM Group.

 Gordon Wade, a Harvard graduate, is an alumnus of P&G's marketing department and the founding partner of the EMM Group. He has consulted globally on consumer marketing for over 30 years. He lives in Florida with his wife Jill and German Shepherd Sara.

 Sat Duggal is one of the world's leading consultants in the systemization of marketing and its enablement through IT. With a career spanning marketing with Unilever and IT Consulting with IBM, he has led the development and implementation of EMM systems at many global F-500 companies. He is a Senior Partner at EMM Group and lives in California with his wife Sonia.

Jeff Saperstein is a marketing consultant and author. For more, check out *www.creatingregionalwealth.com*.

Foreword

The traditional mass-marketing model is broken and in desperate need of repair. Marketers must take into account that people are consuming media in a dramatically different fashion than 10 years ago. Consumers are rapidly changing and so are the ways in which they interact with marketing. When given the choice, they are withholding permission from marketers who continue to embrace the old "intrude and annoy" harassment marketing approach.

Marketers realize we must change how we present our brands to consumers, but many of us aren't changing fast enough or moving in the right direction. Through our involvement with the ANA, P&G has begun working with other thought leaders to help create a new marketing approach in these rapidly changing times. This provocative book captures many of the concepts in which we believe: (1) the mindset that "the Consumer is Boss"; (2) the focus on the marketing process for ensuring plans reflect vital consumer insights; (3) the use of technology to unleash creativity, innovation, and growth in marketing; and (4) the absolute necessity of measuring each component of the marketing demand creation mix.

The principles espoused in this book will help the industry create the right mindset for change. Ignore them at your peril. Our industry owes a great debt to the ANA for leading us toward a new marketing approach. I applaud the publishing of *The New Marketing Mission* by the principals at EMM Group, who are the ANA's thought partners in this critical area.

All of us in the marketing profession need to rethink how we deliver value to our bosses: the consumer and our stakeholders, including for many of us, retailers. This book will help all of us navigate these changing and challenging times.

Jim Stengel,
Global Marketing Officer, Procter & Gamble,
and Chairman, ANA

Preface

Picture a kind, elderly woman. She might be your mother, aunt, or a neighbor down the street. She might live in Des Moines, Munich, or Hong Kong. She might be a teacher, a government employee, or a widow. What distinguishes this person is that she owns stock, either through her pension or a self-directed IRA, and depends on return on her investments to sustain her financial security and quality of life. We wrote this book and dedicate our professional energies to this person, whom we call the shareholder. Our mission is to increase the return on investment (ROI) for this person and the millions of shareholders around the world who have faith in the management and competitive vitality of well-known and respected businesses.

Our confidence in security was shaken on September 11, 2001. In a similar way (although not as tragic and fatal as 9-11), our shareholder experienced the shock of the corporate scandals involving WorldCom, Enron, and other corporate managements who betrayed the trust of their investors. Other scandals have followed, including questionable mutual funds trading practices (more shock for pension owners). We believe our continued quality of life and the future for our children and grandchildren depend on the ability of the global corporation to be trustworthy and innovative, while rewarding the faith of their shareholders with a solid return on their investments. The marketing function has a central role to play in the financial performance and global competitiveness of our major corporations.

ENTERPRISE MARKETING MANAGEMENT IS THE THIRD REVOLUTION IN BUSINESS PRODUCTIVITY

We contend that today the marketing function is fundamentally flawed. We believe it must be transformed before it can become the next revolution to increase business productivity. If desktop computing was the first revolution, and supply chain management using Enterprise Resource

Planning (ERP) systems was the second, then Enterprise Marketing Management (EMM) is the third. As we will profile in this book, major global corporations such as P&G, Kimberly-Clark, IBM, and SAP have begun to re-engineer the marketing function to increase the return on investment. We will provide the views of some of the most successful global marketing professionals as they testify to the transformation of marketing through the integration of process and technology that we propose to you.

Our point is that you need to believe with almost a sense of religious conviction that marketing is different today; we have reached a tipping point, the older ways of doing things are not working anymore. The old marketing model is broken—it was one which shunned the very process, metrics, and technology that drove the productivity revolution on the supply side, preferring instead ad hoc creativity and mass media investments unfettered by any ROI standards.

The revolution starts with marketing as the engine for creating value and brand building as the purpose of marketing. What Enterprise Marketing Management offers is a systematic way for marketing to create value by building brands. Think of brands as financial entities, as opposed to a logo on a package or storefront; the brand drives cash flow and revenue growth.

Now you have a financial concept that the CFO can look at and say, "What is our portfolio of brands? Which of them are generating what kinds of cash flows? Which one seems to return the highest level on investment?" And the CFO can then make decisions about allocations—not just in marketing investment, but also in the capital investment to generate the innovations that sustain brand equity, and to understand a marketing mix model that holds marketing accountable for the return on each dollar spent. So, the marketing investment becomes a financial entity at least equal in stature to building a plant or acquiring a new subsidiary.

THE BUSINESS OF MARKETING

We marketers are in the business of satisfying human needs. If there were an index for measuring the importance of marketing in society, you would surely see a very high correlation between marketing and the quality of life. This is because marketing addresses real customer needs and encourages innovation, which raises the quality of life. Marketing is the engine for improving the quality of life. We see marketing as a profession that enables the entire society to have its manifold needs met in a more efficacious manner. Therefore, we are proud to be marketers.

What Kind of Person Should Choose Marketing As a Profession?

You as marketers have to like satisfying customer needs in a competitive environment. You should be a curious person, a lifelong learner. If you are a person who enjoys learning, who gets a certain thrill out of understanding or has an attitude of "I don't know and I need to find it out," if you like to work across a range of disciplines, if you like competition, and enjoy creativity, then this is a profession for you.

We believe the young people who are entering the marketing profession today have a great opportunity to unleash their creativity and innovate, to create wealth for themselves, for their companies, for shareholders, and for society as a whole.

Our Mission and Hope for the Marketing Profession

EMM Group is dedicated to providing a proven methodology for building brand equity. We want the marketing function to be as respected a discipline as finance, supply chain management, and the other functions that have profit responsibilities. We do that by providing a simple, practical, and complete process, integrated on the desktop of each employee, and supported by software. We supplement the process with examples of content, guides, or checklists that can provide you with the accumulated wisdom of the best global corporations, so you can actually build brand equity.

Some of the content that powers our marketing process is shown in this book. Our hope is that by adopting the best practices and methods detailed in this book, corporate and marketing management will transform the marketing function, so that companies can better satisfy their loyal customers and keep the faith and confidence of their shareholders. The future of marketing and the growth of our society's economic strength depend on it.

Acknowledgments

We would like to thank Jeff Saperstein who organized, bird-dogged, and enhanced our material in its many stages of development. Our gratitude to Vanessa Moore for production management, Lawrence Hargett for copyediting, Anamika Ghosh and Camilla Burg for their diligent organization and research skills.

There are many people who contributed their time, talents, perspectives, and energy to this project. Special thanks to Don E Schultz, Jane Boulware, Elio Leoni-Sceti, Dave Bradley, Peter Sealey, and Jim Speros for their interviews.

We are especially grateful to Jim Stengel, Global Marketing Officer of the Procter & Gamble Company, for his encouragement and collaboration as well as the leadership he is providing the industry in his role as the incoming Chairman of the Association of National Advertisers.

We would also like to add our acknowledgment to all our good friends at SAP and Kimberly-Clark for their pioneering role in the real business of enterprise marketing management.

We wish to acknowledge the help of our colleague, Trini Amador, and also Betsy Farner, the CFO of EMM Group for her patience and diligence.

Our gratitude to the Association of National Advertisers for their support and confidence to sponsor and encourage our project. Special acknowledgment to Barbara Bacci-Mirque and Michelle Hunter for their professionalism in moving forward the discipline of marketing.

Finally, we would like to thank Bob Liodice, President of the ANA, for his personal strength and beneficial influence in making the ANA the powerful supporter of brand owners' interests that it is today.

Hunter Hastings
Gordon Wade
Sat Duggal

Introduction

This book is about growth and the systemic transformation of the marketing function that is required to spur and sustain growth.

Much has been written recently about the pandemic growth crisis afflicting every company and category. As one pundit put it, "If you're not growing, the challenge is to start growing and if you are, it's to keep growing." But in a business environment characterized by mature categories, global competition, and empowered consumers with a "low bidder wins" customer mind-set, consistent core growth is more than merely difficult: it is the paramount challenge for business leaders of the 21st century.

Peter Drucker, one of the most respected management thinkers of the 20th century, once said that the only two functions that can truly grow a business are innovation and marketing. We believe businesses that adopt the approach we propose in this book will unleash the continuous profitable growth all shareholders demand by the synergistic combination of process, metrics, and technology. It will also put the fun and professional fulfillment back into marketing as a profession.

This is reflected in the transformation underway in the broader business community. MIT Sloan School of Management professor Thomas W. Malone has stated this transformation succinctly: "For the first time in history, technologies allow us to gain the economic benefits of large organizations, like economies of scale and knowledge, without giving up the human benefits of small ones, like freedom, creativity, motivation, and flexibility . . . We need to shift our thinking from command-and-control to coordinate-and-cultivate."[1]

We agree . . . but there's a problem. To most CEOs, marketing is an enigma wrapped in a mystery and shrouded in secrecy. Most CEOs come from a nonmarketing background (finance, operations, sales, etc.) and approach marketing with all the enthusiasm of someone entering a dark cave. Many have concluded that marketing is an arcane exercise in episodic creativity that is as manageable and predictable as an outbreak of sunspots. They have embraced the idea that marketing is an art, something much like music or abstract painting. Therefore, they believe good marketing cannot be measured or taught, it can only be appreciated like a fine wine.

DEBUNKING THE MYTH OF MARKETING AS AN ART

This is a myth—a myth that this book is dedicated to shattering. One of the world's premiere marketing companies is Procter & Gamble (P&G). Since 2000, P&G has accelerated its lead over competitors in virtually every category. How? By combining process, technology, and metrics to unleash growth. We know because we had a ringside seat as this vision was turned into reality. P&G had the marketing vision to transform the company from a lumbering giant in the 1990s to a nimble global entrepreneur over the past several years. They did it by applying process, metrics, and technology behind marketing their greatest asset—their brands. This marketing-led growth inspired us to start the EMM Group with the mission of bringing this capability to all marketers in all companies in every vertical.

THE NEW MARKETING MISSION

What are the core beliefs of this new marketing mission?

Primarily, that marketing is a process that is capable of yielding predictable reproducible outputs, not an art whose creative lava flows from the unpredictable eruptions of some magical volcano manned by an itinerant Merlin. The marketing process we espouse is as reliable as grandma's recipe for chocolate cake. It has ordered steps, known and readily obtainable ingredients, well-defined metrics, relevant best practices, and success models.

Ironically, most of the nonmarketing trained CEOs believe in process for every other aspect of their company's activities. Not one of these CEOs would deny the value of a process in manufacturing a medicine, delivering goods through a supply chain, or closing the loop in the order- shipping-billing cycle. Indeed, many have spent millions on software from vendors such as SAP who have captured these processes in software so that every employee can follow the proven, prescribed steps.

Why haven't these same CEOs demanded a process in the marketing function? The standard answer is that process stifles the creativity marketers need and want. The litany goes like this: if you require that my team and I follow a rigid process, you will get a poor creative product and run off all the talented people in the department. At the same time, these marketing apologists will decry the hours and the pace at which the marketing department is working. They will point to high turnover, "burn out," and poor morale, while they denounce the evils of process.

Our response is simple: process is a defense against chaos. It does not stifle creativity; it creates the environment in which people have the time for focused creativity that can move a project in the proper strategic direction. Process protects against substandard output, against re-work, against the all-night sweatshop environment caused by a shoddy or non-existent marketing process.

MIT professor Thomas Malone echoes these principles for the broader business environment. He provides a very powerful argument why standards and procedures actually liberate creativity for innovation. He calls it *The Paradox of Standards*:

> "Rigid standards in the right parts of a system can enable much more flexibility and decentralization in the other parts of the system."

When people make their own decisions, however, establishing coherent standards becomes critical. On the Internet, for example, rigid technical standards—in the form of the underlying Internet Protocols—enable a tremendous amount of flexibility throughout the system. The "managers" of the Internet act as facilitators by defining the protocols. Then anyone using the Internet can easily interact with anyone else to achieve his or her goals.

The standards paradox applies inside companies, too. When you have clear standards for the kind of people you hire and promote, for instance, you can often delegate many decisions to them. And when you have clear standards for evaluating people's results, you don't have to spend a lot of time reviewing and second-guessing their decisions.[2]

Reduce time spent in reviewing and avoid second-guessing decisions? Anyone involved with the marketing function only dreams of such liberation!

THE MARKETING PROCESS MAP CHALLENGE

Here is a challenge to every CEO, COO, and CFO reading this book. Go to your computer or your desk. Pull up your marketing process map. If you have one (and we doubt you do), show us an example of each interconnected step across that continuum completed in a proper way. Show us a template, a guide, or a checklist that you could hand to a new employee with any confidence that she could produce a result up to your standards.

It should not surprise you to learn that not one of the dozens of companies that we benchmarked during our creation of the P&G-inspired Emmperative ASP could meet that test.

This remarkable situation puts marketers and their CEOs in the unique position of tolerating substandard output and repeated rework that no manufacturing professional, no accounting professional, and no logistics professional would ever tolerate. That is why the marketing function needs a process that can raise capabilities and thereby increase the quality of the output and reduce the quantity of rework.

HOW WE ORGANIZED THIS BOOK

In this book, we have provided you with a conceptual framework and a step-by-step approach to transforming your marketing function. In addition, we have a website (*www.newmarketingmission.com*) that provides you with the figures and charts from the book in PDF format that you can download. We have also provided resources, examples of communications, and more detail for you to utilize in your own program.

This book is organized around the step-by-step process that starts with customer insights and then radiates outward to inform every succeeding step. Putting insights at the center is more than a graphic convenience. It dramatizes the intellectual importance of seeking that profound understanding of customer needs that creates competitive advantage.

In addition to insights, each step in the process is required to deliver against metrics appropriate to that step. The ultimate metric of the marketing process is building brand equity.

The creation, nurturing, and enhancement of brand equity are uniquely the job of marketing. While every major function within a company can contribute to building brand equity, only marketing has this goal as its primary functional responsibility.

In the later chapters we will enlarge upon the meaning of brand equity and the ways the marketing process and its associated functional metrics build brand equity. We have organized the book in four sections around these principles and provided many charts, illustrations, case studies, and extended comments from the top marketing people of P&G, Kimberly-Clark, IBM, Ernst & Young, and Reckitt Benckiser, as well as insights from top theorists in the field. Specifically:

In Part I we briefly describe the opportunities, problems, and solutions for marketing. Chapter 1 examines the opportunities and problems with the marketing function as it is now practiced. Chapter 2 details end-to-end content with end-to-end technology to show you how our system works.

In Part II we provide a brand-building process based on customer insights. These include Chapter 3, "Insights: The Heart of the Brand," Chapter 4, "Domain Strategy: A Powerful Growth Stimulus for Brands in Every Industry," Chapter 5, "Building Brand Equity: Brand Vision and Brand Challenge," and Chapter 6, "Long-Term Equity Plan: Brand Imperatives."

In Part III we show you how long-term brand goals become turned into annual plans with initiatives and programs. This section includes Chapter 7, "Building a Plan with an Integrated Marketing Strategy," and Chapter 8, "Functional Excellence."

In Part IV we provide our approach to marketing metrics, technology enablement, and change management. This section includes Chapter 9, "Marketing Metrics: Brand Equity Is Money," Chapter 10, "Technology-Enabled Enterprise Marketing Management," Chapter 11, "The Marketing Knowledge Center," and Chapter 12, "Training: The Fastest Way to Gain Competitive Advantage."

Finally, Chapter 13, "What Should You Do on Monday Morning?" begins to implement our system with a simple five-step approach that starts you on your way.

Our central message is this: *building brand equity is how marketing drives revenue growth and increases the ROI of all marketing activities.* If this sounds likes circular reasoning, it is. When you focus on building brand equity with the process, technology, and metrics discussed herein, you will build equity, and as you build equity you will accelerate your revenue growth, increase your marketing ROI, and increase profitability. Brands with high equity inevitably grow faster and without exception generate higher profit and higher marketing ROI in the medium and longer term.

THE RIGHT METRICS GUIDE THE PROCESS

Increasing brand equity is the goal. We advocate the aggressive use of metrics at every step in the process. The discussion of metrics and their centrality in marketing inevitably results in the response that marketers already have sophisticated metrics in abundance (i.e., cost per thousand messages delivered, cost per sales call, cost per thousand coupons delivered, etc.). The problem with these metrics is that they are input measures. Our processes require that you measure outputs, preferably the ratios of inputs to outputs. In other words, the issue is not what you paid for the messages delivered on X show at Y time; the real issue is the effect that expenditure had on an output such as revenue growth.

In a recent presentation to Wall Street analysts, P&G revealed their determination to require metrics for every marketing decision they make. We had embraced this same approach some two years earlier. We knew that one of the reasons for P&G's embrace of a metric-driven approach was the conviction that the old marketing model had collapsed leading them toward the development of the new "integrated marketing model" approach espoused in this book. Management at P&G realized that the collapse of the old mass-marketing model with its full array of relatively meaningless input metrics meant that the new "integrated" marketing model that was evolving would require new relevant output-oriented metrics. What is so extraordinary about this strategic transformation at P&G is that the old model and its metrics had largely been invented, refined, and promulgated throughout the packaged goods marketing field as the P&G way. In essence, P&G walked away from their own model to evolve a new, dynamic, integrated model with better metrics.

We know—the mere mention of metrics and modeling sends some people in search of an aspirin bottle, but very few things are as important as the ability of marketers to develop models of the relative efficiency and effectiveness of marketing expenditure "A" versus marketing expenditure "B." This is a rapidly developing area of marketing proficiency, one that is undervalued and inadequately practiced by most marketers today.

The need for adequate metrics is driven by the understandable obsession of the CFO for proof of an ever-increasing marketing ROI. This obsession reflects the relative ease of developing an ROI for most discretionary expenditures in any corporate function *except* marketing. Recently, the CFO's appetite for marketing ROI measures has been sharpened by the ability of marketers to calculate ROIs on some Internet- and CRM-related activities. But these are minuscule expenditures compared to mass campaigns on TV and in print and, in business-to-business fields, the cost of a direct sales force. On these major expenditures, ROI is MIA (missing in action).

EVERY MARKETING DECISION WILL BE SUBJECT TO SOME FORM OF MEASUREMENT

In our view, marketers will be forced to embrace the position advocated by P&G's management that every marketing decision be subject to some form of measurement. The operative words here are "some form." Everyone understands that perfect measures are not available for many decisions, but this cannot be used to justify the recalcitrance toward developing relative measures of output efficiency.

In the long run, the marketplace will discredit those who are resistant to metrics and modeling. No other aspect of marketing has made such rapid theoretical and practical advances as metrics and modeling, but many firms continue to look through the rearview mirror or glance ahead and see only excuses for not proceeding.

Marketing cannot avoid measurement forever.

And this brings us to the last leg on the marketing stool—technology. No function in business, with the possible exception of human resource management, has been so lacking in technological enhancement as marketing. Even simple technologies such as the creation of a marketing knowledge center capable of automatically "pushing" a best practice document to a marketer when she mentions it in an e-mail or in a project, is virtually nonexistent today. As a result, marketers often waste hours looking for basic marketing documents relevant to a current work project.

Why marketers would resist sophisticated integrated marketing processes embedded in a shared collaborative environment is astounding.

Perhaps they are fearful of having their prerogatives undermined by a computer.

Let's be clear!

A computer program alone is no substitute for creativity. But using software to create a best practice process and provide the right document at the right time is a major enhancement to the current marketing management practices that are wasteful and inefficient.

THE NEW MARKETING MISSION IS NOW

Now is the time for processes, metrics, technology, and software to be designed for the way marketers work and to be modular and flexible so they will adapt to new information, situations, and understanding of marketing challenges. Once this occurs, marketers will have the free time to create the new product, the new service, or the new idea that makes the profession so satisfying. Marketers want to make things happen to move their brands ahead—so it always was, and so it will be!

If all this sounds like a futuristic pipedream, you should know that such a system was built in 2000 and is being refined and adapted with our clients today. Any company seriously engaged in the new marketing mission will have a major competitive advantage. Importantly, marketing will be fun again and attract bright, creative, energetic people who want to make a difference in the quality of our lives and society.

ENDNOTES

1. Malone, Thomas W. *The Future of Work*, Boston: Harvard Business School Press, 2004.
2. Ibid.

part I

MARKETING: TODAY AND TOMORROW

Marketing is the most important corporate capability because it drives growth. This section highlights just how badly marketing is broken today and discusses the huge business potential that is unleashed if the process is fixed.

Chapter 1

What Is Right and Wrong with Marketing?

Chapter 2

What's New: End-to-End Content Multiplied by End-to-End Technology

WHAT IS RIGHT AND WRONG WITH MARKETING?

> ➤ *What role can the marketing function play in corporate strategic planning?*
> ➤ *How can marketing create shareholder value?*
> ➤ *What's the relationship between brand equity and financial returns?*
> ➤ *How can increasing brand loyalty lead to increased profitability?*

Marketing can solve the biggest challenge that CEOs face: driving and sustaining real top-line revenue growth. But to do so requires the commitment of the CEO and the management team to turn marketing into a powerful business-building tool. How? By demanding the same systematization in marketing as in the other business processes in the corporation. Systematization enables the measurement of return on investment (ROI) in business processes. This, in turn, enables corporations to focus investments in projects that increase ROI and shareholder value.

THE ROLE OF MARKETING

Taken in its historical perspective, on a broad societal level, marketing has been the engine for improving the quality of life. Through constant innovation and development of products, distribution, and communications systems, the quality of life for the average person in the Western world—where modern marketing has been in effect for the past 60 years—has improved dramatically. No one in today's middle class would want to trade places with the richest people at the turn of the 20th century, who did not have the benefits of modern hygiene, transportation, technology, communications, and health care that we take for granted.

Taken in the context of the modern global corporation, marketing has the potential to become a driving force for creating capital appreciation. Unfortunately, the marketing function as practiced today has not lived up to its promise.

There are two fundamental truths we wish to propagate in the transformation of the marketing function as we know it.

1. The single most important strategic objective for any corporation is to build brand equity. The easiest way to understand the significance of brand equity is to recognize that brand loyalty is a function of higher brand equity. The two correlate. The cultivation of the loyalty of customers is the most important and easily measured objective for which you can hold your marketing people accountable. If you attain high consumer loyalty through a strong brand equity, then better profit margins, longer profit life cycles, more successful innovations and generations of long-term growth are sure to follow.

2. Technology has evolved to where it can be useful in supporting marketing processes in a way that would have been inconceivable just 10 years ago. It is now easier to integrate the best practices of the best companies in the world onto the desktop of every marketer, in every operating division, in every corner of the globe.

Our objective is to show you how this can be done, and to illustrate how the best global companies are implementing this now.

WHAT'S THE OPPORTUNITY?

The opportunity on which we focus in this book is growth. Specifically, we will describe a complete process whereby corporations big and small can create predictable revenue growth streams over a multiple-year horizon.

We refer to real revenue growth: more customers, buying even more of your products and services and at even higher prices, as you find ever greater levels of value to deliver to them.

Typically, the processes we describe can generate higher levels of gross margin. You can achieve this goal through the same process of identifying higher levels of customer value, and by changing the marketing mix of offerings to the consumer, removing or de-emphasizing the lower-margin, lower-value delivery items and adding higher-margin, higher-value delivery items.

While our processes alone do not directly deliver shareholder value, there is typically a very high correlation between the independent variables of consistent revenue growth and rising gross margins, and the dependent variable of shareholder value. A lot of other factors can intervene and have an effect on that dependent variable, including how well the corporation utilizes its assets, the state of its borrowing, and a range of financial and governance issues that affect Wall Street sentiment. But overall, the correlation between driving revenue growth and gross margins and the creation of shareholder value is usually high enough to merit a CEO's and a CFO's focus on the processes we propose.

We will demonstrate another correlation, between growth in brand equity and growth in shareholder value.

Some of the recent literature about enterprise growth has been concerned with "disruptive technologies" and "new to the world" innovation. Those are interesting phenomena, but they are not what sustain growth in corporations, businesses, and brands. And even the doctors of disruption advise executives to meet investor expectations by "making better products that can be sold for more money to attractive, that is, demanding and high-end, customers . . . and to do so consistently with processes that transform inputs into . . . greater value."[1] We focus on sustainable growth in our processes. There is no need for global corporations to completely re-engineer their value chains, restructure their companies, and revamp their organizations. Companies can systematically transform and make the changes to achieve the "agility" that growth requires.

BRAND-BUILDING IS THE WISEST INVESTMENT FOR SUSTAINABLE GROWTH

The established corporation can leverage many assets for growth, but we want to highlight just one of them throughout this book: their brands. Brands are assets that can get stronger with time. They represent a historical accumulation of investment in the form of marketing spending, distribution, R&D, plus the knowledge and energy of the people who have worked to build the brand over time. Usually, the longer a brand has been in existence, the better.

For example, consider Budweiser beer. No brand-naming specialist today would consider giving a beer product—which by definition must be fresh and contemporary to appeal to its young (but, of course, legal drinking age) consumers—such a bizarre and old-fashioned sounding name. But the brand has survived attacks by light beer, imported beer, stronger beer, better-tasting beer, more humorous beer, private label beer, local beer, craft beer, and many other competitors to the beverage category such as wine coolers, soft drinks, and bottled water. Bud and Bud Light nevertheless hold a higher share of the U.S. domestic market than they have ever had before (50 percent market share by the fourth quarter, 2003). They are growing their international business, and Anheuser-Busch, the brand owner, has been able to deliver consistent growth in revenue and earnings in a market where all other contenders (including larger, and very highly accomplished corporations like the former Philip Morris, now Altria) have struggled and, in many cases, failed.

On the business-to-business side, take IBM as an example. The now-retired chairman, Louis H. Gerstner, used biting irony when he turned a scathing phrase, often used by misguided "dot commers" to disparage large corporations, into the title of his book about the turnaround of the IBM corporation: *Who Says Elephants Can't Dance*. Mr. Gerstner is a great simplifier and he made a very short list of the most important elements of his turnaround plan. Two of them were the importance of leveraging the massive historical investment in the IBM brand, and a single-minded focus on customers and their needs. These are the very foundations all marketers should construct for their business development.

Brands and customers . . . If August Busch and Lou Gerstner, two of the most successful CEOs of our time, can master these two ideas, why can't all other CEOs?

One plausible reason may be that many CEOs, who ascended the corporate ladder from finance, operations, legal, mergers and acquisitions (M&A), and the corporate suite, do not fully appreciate the very simple equation that *building brand equity builds shareholder value.*

Here's how the equation works. The equity in brands exists entirely in customers' minds. Brands, whether they be products or services, are the sum of the perceptions, past and present, significant and trivial, that consumers hold based on the totality of their experiences with the brand including the usage experience, its advertisements, its human representatives, and so on.

Customers who hold strongly favorable perceptions overwhelmingly award the brand with more frequent purchase and usage, and with greater loyalty (i.e., a higher percentage of their requirements are filled by the brand). These customers require less promotion and price incentive, and are therefore more profitable to the corporation. They recommend the brand to their friends and become a low-cost and highly persuasive marketing campaign all their own. They are highly receptive to their favorite brand's expansion into adjacent areas of need, and so make the introduction of new products and services by the brand faster, cheaper, and more profitable. As we will show in Chapter 4 regarding domain strategy, one of the great advantages of strong brands is their capacity to introduce products and services outside of a narrow category description. They can be positioned as leaders in new, innovative, emergent niches that have greater growth and profitability potential. Brand loyalty can be understood in financial terms as "goodwill." Goodwill is the difference between the brand value and hard assets. The brand is an asset, but it does not appear on the balance sheet. For example, Olay is now a vast array of products, all on a single advertising platform. And the value of that brand has multiplied from when it was simply a functional moisturizing cream.

So, brand loyalty leads directly to higher market shares, faster growth, valuable competitive differentiation, and economies of scale. These benefits translate directly into shareholder value.

A number of studies have been completed in support of this simple, powerful relationship between brand equity and shareholder value. One of the well-known studies is from Stern Stewart,[2] the econometricians who popularized the measure called EVA (economic value added) as the single metric with which CEOs could guide their financial strategy. They selected the Young & Rubicam BrandAsset Valuator (BAV) methodology as the basis for measuring brand equity, and their own EVA methodology for analyzing financial performance. The data yields a correlation score of greater than 0.6 (pretty high in statistical terms) between the two variables. Excerpts from their study included in the BrandEconomics white paper are provided below.

BrandAsset Valuator and EVA

The BAV model documents the evolving relationship that a brand has with consumers. The relationship begins with differentiation (D); followed by the other attributes, relevance (R), esteem (E), and knowledge (K). Plotting a brand's performance on these four dimensions generates a "pillar pattern" that provides a powerful diagnostic of the stage of development of a brand. The height of a pillar is a brand's percentile rank among all competitive brands in its country.

Differentiation and relevance act as leading indicators of brand health while esteem and knowledge are lagging indicators. Stern Stewart combines differentiation and relevance to form a composite figure for brand strength, and combines esteem and knowledge to form a composite figure for brand stature. The resulting "power grid," shown in Figure 1.1, is a diagnostic framework for analyzing brand health.

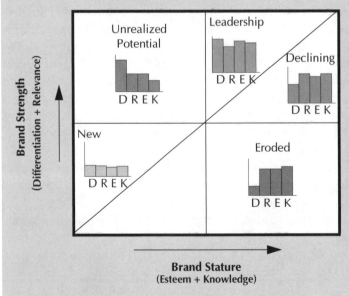

FIGURE 1.1   Brand strength/stature grid.

Using this model, Stern Stewart was able to link consumer franchise to value creation in a systematic, objective way, as shown in Figure 1.2.

Monobrands with at least 5% change in D&R over 2 years.

	R Declined	R Grew
D Grew	Δ EVA = $322m 20.1% annual NOPAT growth	Δ EVA = $435m 23.7% annual NOPAT growth
D Declined	Δ EVA = ($149m) 13.3% annual NOPAT growth	Δ EVA = $86m 15.3% annual NOPAT growth

FIGURE 1.2   Monobrands and change in differentiation and relevance.

Some of the significant results of the study are as follows:

1. A large part of the intangible value of companies in certain sectors can be explained by the health of their brand as measured by BAV.
2. In a brand context, you rarely gain in volume what you sacrifice in margin.
3. Brands that suffered declines in both their differentiation and relevance (bottom left quadrant) still reported increased operating profit (NOPAT, net operating profit after tax) despite declining EVA. This reflects their inability to sustain the returns needed to justify the cost of the additional capital invested in the business.

Peter Doyle of the University of Warwick has published numerous studies on the subject of shareholder value creation via brand building. His approach focuses on the value of future cash flows from branding that result from customer loyalty.

> The objective of brand strategy should be . . . to maximize shareholder value. Value is determined by expectations about the present value of the long-term cash flow the strategy will generate.
>
> Successfull branding impacts on cash flow are:
>
> ▶ Increasing the level of cash flow
> ▶ Accelerating the level of cash flow
> ▶ Extending the duration of cash flow
> ▶ Reducing the risk attached to future cash flow
>
> The task is to exploit these advantages so as to increase the present value of the brand's future cash flow.[3]

See the book's website, *www.newmarketingmission.com*, for the links to the Stern Stewart study.

A study by Gruca and Rego[4] examined the impact of customer satisfaction on a firm's operational cash flows, a key determinant of shareholder value. As managers seek to link their activities to the measure of most concern to top management, this study offered important evidence that investment in customer satisfaction represents resources well spent: satisfied customers are central to creating shareholder value.

These are just a few of the recent studies supporting the case for brand building and increasing customer loyalty as providing a solid foundation for superior return on investment. The sources and the data are impeccable. Yet there is relatively little appreciation of the phenomenon in the C-Suite—the offices of the CEO, CFO, and COO. Few corporations have a CMO—chief marketing officer—and those that do often do not treat that position as the equal of the other denizens of the C-Suite. Business unit and division presidents tend not to be focused on brand building. And yet, it would seem reasonable to surmise that if the C-Suite understood that brand equity drives shareholder value or, more simply, that brand equity drives profit, growth, and sales, they would be intensely focused on ensuring that their company has a world-class capability to build brands and brand equity, and to do so in a manner that is competitively advantaged, repeatable, effective, and efficient.

SHIFT IN THE MARKETING FUNCTION: ENTER THE CHIEF MARKETING OFFICER

The creation of the true Chief Marketing Officer role is important to the changes we propose for the marketing and brand-building function.

Marketing must become a value center instead of a cost center. The driver is the elevation of marketing to the more fundamental role of brand building.

Today, marketing is thought of narrowly as research, new product development, communications, and sales support. It is an artifact of the marketing department, and sometimes (such as in many high-tech companies) the "marketing communications" department—the title alone is an emasculation.

Brand building, on the other hand, is a much more fundamental activity. Brands are financial assets. Their value is computed by Interbrand and paraded on the front cover of *Business Week*. Soon, brands will be captured on balance sheets as assets and their values will be scrutinized by Wall Street. Brand health also drives EPS (earning per share) because a growing brand commanding a premium price and customer loyalty is a profit machine, representing an earnings stream that can be projected into the future with confidence.

And, as is fitting for an activity that can drive both the balance sheet and the P&L, brand building (formerly marketing) is an activity that should command the attention of the entire C-Suite—the CEO, COO, CFO, and CIO, as well as the CMO.

The chief marketing officer title has been recently minted but is seldom associated with the true C-Suite role we propose for the position. The CMO title should command the same stature as the other CXO titles. The CFO and CIO run mission-critical functions—ensuring that the economic engine of the enterprise is perfectly tuned and the technological underpinnings of the enterprise are optimized and, ideally, competitively advantaged. The company can't succeed without these functions performing at the highest levels of effectiveness every day.

The COO pulls it all together and ensures the right allocations of the right resources for best corporate performance, while the CEO focuses on strategy and shareholder value. In the corporate environment we see today, the CMO plays a secondary role; if his/her budget has to be cut in the fourth quarter to accommodate more pressing needs, then so be it. In our current business environment, marketing just isn't as important as finance, technology, or operations.

But this should not be so! Today, there is nothing more important or more fundamental to the health of the enterprise than the health of its brands (or of the corporation as a brand). And the CMO is the creator, manager, monitor, and guardian of the brand.

The CMO must understand the balance sheet and EPS leverage of the brand, and must take responsibility for the future cash flow implications of brand health. Insofar as the brand must be represented by every individual in the enterprise—every call center operator, every shipping clerk who affects timely delivery, every IT employee who affects whether systems properly support brand performance, as well as every salesperson and marketing practitioner—then the CMO must be able to speak persuasively to those individuals and inspire them in their role of delivering the brand to the customer every day. The CMO must also become a marketing technologist and understand how technology can support the processes that enable brand building to succeed.

The CMO must assume a role that is not only equal to his/her peers in the C-Suite, but in some ways ascendant. Certainly, brand building must receive new levels of respect and support from finance, for example. Where, previously, marketing was dinged for budget compliance, now there must be a collaborative effort to develop financial models to link marketing spending to returns and measure the financial performance of the brand asset. Where, previously, marketing was the stepchild of an IT department focused on running the factory floor and the order-taking system, now IT must support the breakthrough enterprise marketing management systems designed to maximize the productivity of brand assets.

The discussion in corporate boardrooms should now concentrate on *brand building*. At EMM Group, where we focus on human, financial, and technological systems for maximizing brand development, we find ourselves working in fields as diverse as consumer goods, financial services, pharmaceuticals, high tech, retail, and automotive. As a value center, brand building is fundamental to all these industries. There is no difference—all are brand-focused, all are marketing-driven.

And now the CMO must be empowered to step up to take center stage, with all the opportunity and responsibility that goes with it. A beautiful scenario. However . . .

This is not the case in most global corporations today. Why? It's partly because the C-Suite undervalues brand equity, but also because the C-Suite does not understand that building brand equity is the marketing department's primary responsibility. Marketing has not been viewed as a serious business discipline. It does not have the bottom-line accountability and prestige of finance, M&A, enterprise resource planning, value chain management, manufacturing, logistics, technology, or data processing. For the most part, marketers have brought this upon themselves.

JUST WHAT IS THE PROBLEM WITH MARKETING?

Marketing, as it is practiced today in most corporations, developed as an arcane art and not a management science. It can be characterized by three I's:

- Inspiration (as opposed to process)
- Individuals (as opposed to corporate capability)
- Inconsistency (as a result of the two above points)

Inspiration: Marketers tend to define their art as a realm of *ideas* (another "I" word). Where do these ideas come from? Not—heaven forbid—from any process that could be taught or codified or systematized. No; ideas are sourced in inspiration, and we can't define inspiration except to say that it emanates from certain privileged . . .

Individuals: According to this conventional wisdom, great marketers seem to be born, not made. Certain gurus rise up as superior sources of ideas, having demonstrated inspired prowess in arcana such as advertising or promotion or "buzz." They are to be respected and followed, but they can't be a source of learning because this stuff can't be passed on. It dies when the guru dies, which explains why the results of marketing are marked by such . . .

Inconsistency: Any art that depends on inspiration from unknown sources and is practiced by gurus who can't pass on their wisdom can not be expected to deliver consistent or predictable results. It can be expected only to yield excellent outcomes as a percentage of the effort expended, somewhat like a hitter in baseball. Three out of 10 is a pretty good score when 90 percent of the players don't do quite that well.

Because of these three I's, marketing has not been able to assert itself as a true business discipline. It concentrates on its component parts, and not on the integration of the parts into a whole. As a result, marketing tends to be seen as "advertising," or sometimes "research," or positioning, or segmentation, or (more recently) customer relationship management. Even when marketing is associated with "branding," the image is of things like brand names, logos, style, and dress; that is, attributes rather than core substance. The "buzz" about marketing always runs quickly to tactics—ads, campaigns, sponsorships, pricing, promotions—and seldom focuses on the strategic insight driving the initiatives through the marketing mix. Those brands that do, such as Procter & Gamble (P&G)'s Folgers and Kimberly-Clark's Huggies in packaged goods, and Apple, Dell, and Intel in newer high-tech categories, are richly rewarded.

Most marketing efforts tend to be frenetic rather than organized, opportunistic rather than disciplined. Most CEOs do not use marketing as a strategic tool to build the franchise value. Those who do, such as Lou Gerstner and Jack Welsh, former CEO at General Electric, are also richly rewarded.

MARKETING PROCESS CAN BE INTEGRATED INTO MARKETING SOFTWARE

Another major problem of marketing is that management does not understand how to measure return on marketing investment. So as we move marketing from being an art to a science, we emphasize two things: marketing can be engineered as a process, and each of the components in this process can be measured.

These are the same principles that govern enterprise resource planning (ERP), a well-established business discipline at the "back end" of the enterprise; this is the manufacturing, logistics, and supply chain that enables the enterprise to manufacture and deliver services and products to customers and consumers.

The supply chain is a *process*. Just think what would happen if supply chains were deemed to be the occasional inspiration of individuals. What if the output is unpredictable? What would happen if successful implementation were only 3 times out of 10? Picture what the Wal-Mart buyers would say to a supplier that described its supply chain in this manner, and used it as an excuse to meet delivery windows only 30 percent of the time.

Suppliers to Wal-Mart and other demanding customers subject the supply chain to the rigors of business processes analysis to ensure that unpredictability and human errors do not destroy their ability to do business. The supply chain is broken down into its component steps from beginning to end, guaranteeing consistent, high-quality outcomes. No matter how complex the subject, process mapping and process engineering can reduce it to extremely simple components—individual steps, each of which has an input and an output, plus resources, tools, and enablers to help the process owner to complete the step, and, lastly, measurements to assess whether the step was completed successfully. Each individual step has an owner with a clear responsibility. Suddenly, the step is no longer difficult or mysterious; it is simply a step. Based on your defined role, take the input, use the tools and enablers to execute the step, measure the output, and pass it on to the next step. These steps linked end-to-end become a complete process—predictable, repeatable, and measurable.

Once a process is codified in this manner, another aspect of high productivity becomes possible: the process can be enabled by software. That is what we propose to be the future of the marketing function: processes embedded into software with the focus on the priorities that really matter to build brand equity. It is with this framework that marketers can unleash their creativity and innovation to move their business ahead, to increase top-line revenue and increase shareholder value.

Beyond process issues, there are also broader issues that the future of marketing must address. These are organizational and cultural. We think of the issue as the alignment of marketing processes with marketing structure and culture.

Dr. Don E. Schulz describes the issue in terms of the "demand chain" way of organizing versus the "supply chain" way of organizing.

Interview: Don E. Schultz, Professor, Northwestern University

The first basic problem most organizations have is their structure. They are structured on a functional basis and it does not seem to make a difference where you go or whom you look at, they are still utilizing a manufacturing-based approach. A group of specialists who all report up vertically, competing for turf, money, and power inside the organization—and the customer be damned. The problem is focus on getting rid of products as opposed to how to make this structure work for the customer.

A second problem is the compensation system. As long as we reward people for just getting rid of product, they will never look at the customer.

The processes will not work unless you solve the problem of organizational structure and compensation.

Tesco: Managing a Customer Portfolio, Rather Than a Product Portfolio

A good example is Tesco in the United Kingdom. They focus on capturing customer data. They then provide the products and services their customers want. Tesco uses rewards and incentives to build relationships with customers. They have turned it into a business model. They have a group of consumers who believe in the Tesco brand. That belief has allowed Tesco to enter other business areas much more extensively than competitors can. They have set up an insurance company, a bank, clubs, and a telecommunications business. They understand their customer base and what products and services they want, and then organize businesses around those customers' needs. They are managing millions of customers and not managing 40,000 products—that's where the big difference is.

There will be two future models—the Tesco model of demand chain or the Wal-Mart model of supply chain. You will either become customer focused or supply chain focused.

The Wal-Mart model depends on logistics, computer, and supply chain expertise—marketing has little value. The Tesco model is focused on understanding who the customers are and what they want. Marketing has to focus on the demand chain.

The structure of the customer-focused demand management company is different from the structure of the supply chain–focused management company. And so is the culture. In supply chain–focused companies, efficiency comes first. The values are about saving money and saving time. Often, the customer value proposition is built on price and not on quality. In demand chain focused companies, the values are about brand building, about knowing the customer, understanding the customer, serving the customer, delighting the customer, and keeping the customer loyal. "Living the brand" becomes the culture that links all the employees, their vendors and suppliers, and their customers.

SUMMARY

The function of marketing must be redefined to enhance brand building rather than be viewed as a collection of tactical marketing mix tools. The marketing manager should transform into a chief marketing officer, responsible for creating the processes and integrating the technology that increase brand equity at every touch point with the customer. Marketers must be accountable for the return on investment for their activities. Only then can they earn the right to be equals in the corporate suite.

ENDNOTES

1. Clayton M. Christensen and Michael E. Raynor, *The Innovator's Solution: Creating and Sustaining Successful Growth*, Boston: Harvard Business School Press, 2003.

2. "Bringing New Clarity to Brand Management and Strategy," BrandEconomics LLC White Paper.

3. "Shareholder Value-Based Brand Strategies," Peter Doyle, *Brand Management*, Sept. 2001.

4. "Customer Satisfaction, Cash Flow, and Shareholder Value," Thomas Gruca and Lop Rego, *Marketing Science Institute Working Paper Series*, Issue 2, 2003.

chapter 2

WHAT'S NEW: END-TO-END CONTENT MULTIPLIED BY END-TO-END TECHNOLOGY

➤ *How does the enterprise upgrade its marketing capability to make brand building a core competency?*

➤ *How does the enterprise integrate best practices into all areas of marketing?*

➤ *How is marketing integrated into general management rather than being a functional specialty?*

➤ *How can technology leverage the marketing function?*

➤ *How can the chief information officer (CIO) and the chief marketing officer (CMO) work in concert to increase top-line revenue?*

It is traditional to think of marketing and technology as separate. That's because, historically, they have been. It's another aspect of the classification of marketing as art and not science. The CIO has been called on to support finance, manufacturing, logistics, and even basic research, but not marketing.

Indeed, how could the CIO support marketing? The functions supported to date by technology have invested a lot of resources into systematizing their activities as robust, repeatable processes. Only then can technology be applied to make those processes more efficient and more effective. Process comes before technology, or at least they must be developed simultaneously.

Therein lies one of the main barriers to the marketing revolution we seek to create: marketing resists process, which means that marketing can't easily be supported by technology. Therefore, marketing cannot aspire to be a powerful business system of the same stature as the other functions unless it undergoes a fundamental transformation.

Marketing should integrate knowledge, intelligence, and interpretation: we develop knowledge of our customers, use the intelligence we have developed over time to process that knowledge, and then use the interpretation in strategy, positioning, communications, and execution. We believe that marketing requires a holistic solution of both content and knowledge as well as technology, so that it can benefit from the same productivity solution that technology has provided for supply chain, finance, and other disciplines.

PROCESS IS THE GUARD AGAINST CHAOS

Marketing is a process, just like manufacturing, finance, or any other business activity. It can be enhanced by applying business process engineering or re-engineering. In today's tough market conditions, marketing professionals have a high "burn-out" rate, because fewer people are now involved in the marketing function, and work pressures have increased proportionately upon those few still engaged. In most marketing departments, people seem to be constantly reworking the same problems. Every day marketers are constantly doing rework, constantly doing low-level tasks, and functioning in a "chaotic" workplace. However, they can be transformed by the systematic adoption of proven processes. Marketers should be focused on strategic thinking and activities that will increase shareholder value. Process provides the precondition for progress and helps marketing professionals create real brand equity.

Yet, in marketing, the "P word" (process) is often deemed to be mechanical. There tends to be a lot of resistance from marketers who believe marketing isn't a process, it is an art that should be appreciated. On the contrary, process should be looked upon as a magic elixir, because it provides a framework for creative endeavors to find insights that lead to innovation. Those who resist process are condemning their brands to an endlessly repeated cycle of mediocrity and forcing marketers to perform mundane tasks that do little toward increasing brand equity.

Here is a typical scenario for marketing professionals entering the field:

Imagine a young M.B.A. graduate joining one of the top consumer packaged companies. She has grand visions of launching innovative new brands, repositioning existing brands, and applying all the other great strategic tools that she learned as part of her education. Her grand designs crash to reality very quickly. One of her first tasks is to get approval for a regular run-of-the-mill consumer promotion offer. By no means is this an easy task. The promotion proposal requires 17 signatures from managers in different functions, including senior managers all the way to the president of the business division. She must physically carry the document from desk to desk, taking three weeks of dedicated effort to obtain all the signatures.

The world of marketing is replete with similar stories. Bright young marketers (and certainly some old marketers as well!) are subjected to grindingly menial tasks. Our studies reveal that 50 to 60 percent of the time marketing professionals spend on their job involves unnecessary and low-priority tasks such as checking on the status of ongoing projects, waiting for approvals, and searching for information. Not only is this a tremendous loss of productivity and a misplaced investment of company resources, but it also is highly demotivating for marketing practitioners. Ironically, this process-starved environment *stifles* the very creativity and productivity that every good marketer desires.

THE CASE FOR PROCESS IN MARKETING

With defined processes, creativity can be directed toward improving measured performance. Then it can be objectively evaluated. If we allow process to define the box, creativity can find the outside. If we allow process to set the bar, then creativity can raise it. But if we don't know the dimensions of the box or the bar, we'll never find the outside or the upside. Innovation can only occur in context, and process provides the context and the opportunity for marketing excellence.

An example is the development of the iPod by Apple. This recent product breakthrough is one of the most successful marketing innovations in the music and personal computer business. By following careful market research processes to understand the needs of customers for inexpensive, easy-to-use, personalized music storage systems, and by following focused product design processes in alliance with focused R&D processes that leveraged Apple technology, Apple was able to solve all problems customers experienced with MP3 players, and unleash growth in the category. By following contemporary processes of brand equity leverage, Apple was able to leverage historical brand investments and create an emotional bond with customers built on a solid historical platform. As a result, Apple now sells more iPod units, at a higher profit margin, than personal computers. They got the convenient, personal music brand benefit right, and did so before Sony or the music companies, because they used effective process.

End-to-end process involves every aspect of a brand, from initial concept through production, distribution, and continuous innovation. These are the benefits for end-to-end process adoption in marketing:

Best practice. By standardizing and sharing the achievement of a particular function, like great advertising, the current best practice will be captured. You will not knowingly codify a process that is inferior. And hey, presto! Those who follow your process in your company are working at best practice levels. An example might be the development of strategy briefs and creative copy platforms, which are illustrated by the progression of a successful campaign from concept to implementation.

Springboard from which to leap higher. Having codified best practices as you know it, you have constructed a springboard from which to leap even higher. Marketing practitioners throughout the company, who view and use the process, will volunteer improvements in output quality, speed, and cost. An example could be the directive for innovation in the packaging, servicing, or customer communication for a particular brand that has enhanced customer satisfaction levels.

Viral. Once you embark on enhancement of one process, you are driven to improve the whole marketing process, from end to end and top to bottom. An example might be the realization that, once the brand equity management process is codified, it can be enhanced via the codification of an insights process as an input.

Generates measurable improvement and return on marketing investment (ROMI). Sound process management requires standards, so that current and future marketing generations know how to share excellence across a common platform. While there are many ways to ascertain whether improvements are genuine, the best one is the simplest: Is the output better? ROMI can be tracked only if outputs and inputs are measured, and measurement can be linked to the relevant activity that produced it only if there is a process to join inputs to outputs. An example might be the implementation of point-of-sale materials or channel management incentives that can be replicated for success.

Knowledge and training. Research shows that marketers want on-the-job training they can apply immediately. A well-conceived process that is fully developed and generously presented constitutes some of the best training a corporation can offer. The process, having been distilled from years of experience and the learning that comes from repeated use, represents the accumulated knowledge of the corporation and its experts in the area where the process applies. One example of this is the shopper research conducted by P&G, and the way this information is disseminated for improved merchandising and in-store promotions.

INTEGRATING CONTENT AND TECHNOLOGY

Effective processes require robust content and the technology to make them accessible to approved users across all geographies and all functions in the organization. Our solution supplements a process with examples, guides, and checklists that can provide users with the insights and best practices to enable them to actually build brand equity.

The Case for IT in Marketing

We believe that IT is an important tool that can consistently bring best practices or a process to the people of the corporation—24/7. IT can help to accomplish many universal marketing work process requirements:

1. Provide common process standards and the capability to work over a diverse network at high levels of speed. Everyone can be working off a common set of data that can be instantly arrayed and conveyed to everyone either simultaneously or asynchronously.

2. Provide a common language for understanding, progressing, and revising projects that can be worked on immediately and changed quickly as required.

3. Reduce wasted time by increasing standardization where appropriate, thereby freeing up people and time for creativity.

4. Bring new people on a team up to a very high standard very quickly, because the training is inherent in documents and in the process.

5. Expedite approvals; it can provide the work to be reviewed and approved, circulate automatically, aggregate comments and suggestions, and alert managers to the process of approvals through the chain.

Interview: Dave Bradley, Senior VP, Global Solution Marketing and Field Marketing Services, SAP

Dave Bradley is one of the most qualified executives on the planet to comment on technology for marketing. His career has embraced leading positions in line marketing, consulting and marketing services, pioneering analytics and modeling, as well as leading-edge technologies in systems and software. We talked to him in his position as VP Marketing Management, Global Sales and Distribution at IBM, and again some months later after he had joined SAP as Senior VP, Global Solution Marketing and Field Marketing Services.

Technology will change marketing both internally and externally (by external I mean channel and customer facing).

External

Technology will make companies better able to respond quickly to rapid changes in the marketplace and in competitive realities; it will enable faster cycles in time-to-market and time-to-value; and these new ways of doing business will enable greater and faster asset reuse, and new ways to create value via partnering within a value network.

Collaboration also is enabled across a value net. For example, new ways to gather and process customer insights can be more rapidly processed as inputs to a design team. This is an example of a situation where technology enables marketing—it is not transactional (which is the area of application where technology supported business in the past), but collaborative knowledge management. Specifically, in the auto industry, in the design of an automobile, the <u>manufacturing value chain</u> is already optimized because it is so advanced and so computer based. Now the <u>design chain</u> can be optimized—new customer insights are created by deep data mining, the designer makes a change, and the change cascades through a design collaboration grid so that the chain of supply can be adjusted in minutes, for what was formerly a long cycle change. This transforms the whole cognitive process of design in a collaborative fashion across boundaries. It also changes how designers think and act as a community—like other marketing functions, the "art" of creativity (acts of design based on intuition and individual preference) becomes the science of design (responding to new customer data with a new customer solution in a rapid, closed cycle).

<u>Customer Insights</u>. In companies such as securities firms/brokerages, sophisticated data mining and credit decisioning is being made possible by supercomputers and grid capabilities, which can create powerful new analytics and algorithms. Faster speeds and shared service mean that businesses get their insights faster today and, as they use these capabilities on a larger scale (e.g., linking together the 10,000 PCs that are idle in the corporation), they can create new data models and new insights.

There are two advances that will support the achievement of new data models and insights. One is the ability of grid computing to interconnect databases much more so than is the case today, so that new patterns can be observed and analyzed. A second is the increasing ability to analyze unstructured data and create meaningful output. For example, an IBM service known as Web Fountain can mine web traffic across multiple sites and create a "buzz index" of what people are saying about your product or service. Text analysis around unstructured data (such as comments at a website or voice-to-text of calls to a call center) can be married to structured data (such as sales data) to create new analyses, which were never before possible.

Internal

A major contribution of technology to the science of marketing is the refinement of process.

Internal collaboration is incredibly important to the success of any company. It starts with collaboration around documents (e.g., in "team rooms") and advances to the concept of syndicated content: people produce objects that come together dynamically around audiences. For example, an object might be a framework for a marketing plan or program. It might include a list of elements of a program plan, and the elements are tagged with the attributes that link them to a marketplace theme or to a customer need or to a market need. At the local level, salespeople or marketers identify the profile of the customer or the market in terms of needs, and the plan composes itself dynamically at the local level by mapping marketing plan elements to the local customer need.

This changes workflow completely. Market plans are assembled and composed downstream, closer to the customer. Field sales and customer management never again gets handed down "plans that don't work in my market." Marketing plan elements are "write once, use many times." In an environment of tools, standard processes, and defined objectives, incredible flexibility and customization can be achieved by working in component terms. (*Author's Note: This is the equivalent of MIT Professor Thomas Malone's paradox of standards—rigid standards in the right parts of a system can enable much more flexibility and decentralization in other parts of the system.*)

Proof of Performance and the Marketer-Technologist

SAP delivers proof of business performance for its customers—visible, measurable, demonstrable hard-number proof of the ROI of all kinds of investments and operating expenditures at the business case level. This is becoming more and more necessary for running a business and getting investor and board support—every year, every quarter, every day.

For marketers, SAP develops business software that operates in the context of the business suite—ERP, CRM, and other modules are tightly integrated into operations management, and the underlying data layer ties it all together (e.g., CRM software tied into SAP financial software to provide both financial results and costs and an ROI calculation). Via the software, the customer can define "objects" in business planning (such as a marketing campaign) and link the object to financial results. The outcome is a holistic view of all business activities tied to financial results. The software can measure the response to specific marketing stimuli, groups of expenditures, and so on.

In order for this fundamental capability to work, there must be operating processes that the software can automate and link to financials. The marketing community has not yet invested in the operations capability (i.e., process), and has yet to learn how to apply that operations capability. Yet there is no reason why they can't operate on this level—the enterprise software suite is proven, and the marketing community can have the same capabilities and the same tools as any other business function.

The change that marketing must go through is not only significant from a business process standpoint, it is also significant at the cultural level. Instead of marketing working on their own with their own campaign management databases and spreadsheets, they must change and become plugged in to the "real," central core of business operations and business performance metrics.

Marketing executives must develop a major IT competency in their organization in order to operate effectively at the enterprise, integrated level. They must be able to direct the right investments and initiatives and develop the right competencies without outsourcing it to Central IT. Central IT can direct the overall enterprise architecture but can't be expected to be expert in marketing and proof of performance in marketing. In order to pull this off, marketing must have the process and technology skills within their department, so that they can introduce their needs effectively into the IT strategy of the company.

Gaps in Conventional IT Support for Marketing

Most organizations have used only very basic technology tools to support their marketing operations. Most of these solutions have been either home-grown or developed using third-party providers of point solutions. The traditional suppliers to the marketing process, such as prepress houses and media agencies, have created licensed or hosted applications to help automate processes in their own domain of expertise. However, these technologies have been designed only for addressing part of one process or at best, only one process. They are not scalable and integrated to meet the end-to-end needs of all the marketing processes and do not provide the required content. In fact, one reason why many attempts to institute customer relationship management (CRM) failed is because there was no mapping of the associated process, and no content support. CRM's fatal flaw is that it records interactions with consumers, but is unable to enhance the interaction using knowledge, or to interpret the interaction and make it better.

In the absence of an integrated solution, many of the home-grown and third-party applications are eagerly adopted. However, significant gaps exist in the current IT support for marketing. Some of these key gaps are:

- **No end-to-end coverage.** The current applications are disparate point solutions and don't support end-to-end processes and content.

- **Ad hoc development.** Isolated development has led to point solutions that do not integrate with each other: the consequences include data redundancy, manual entry and re-entry, usability issues in doing work in different places, maintenance issues, and a plethora of additional issues that are typical of a fragmented approach to development for a functional area.

- **Duplicated functionality.** Many applications have components and infrastructure elements that are duplicated, and yet implemented differently.

- **Nonstandard data.** Various examples of inconsistencies in data (e.g., different product hierarchies used by sales and marketing) lead to problems in integrating marketing with the enterprise application infrastructure.

- **Data integration with external data providers.** This is a major problem given the issues of dissimilar product hierarchy, accounting for special deals and other such data integration issues.

These gaps in existing technology for marketing process support are significant. However, this should not be an obstacle for the chief marketing officer (CMO) to achieve his ultimate goal of building brand equity. But how can the CMO harness technology to attain this goal?

INTRODUCING A NEW ROLE—THE MARKETER TECHNOLOGIST

The CMO's job is becoming gargantuan. How will future CMOs grow the most important asset the company has—its brands? By ensuring corporate congruence, so that everyone in the corporation is keeping the brand's promise to its customers.

The CMO must become, as part of the new job description, a never-before-seen hybrid of marketer and technologist—a marketer technologist (MT). One part of the CMO's job is to identify, understand, catalogue, and codify the most effective marketing best practices for brand building; for every customer type in every country and every channel, whether digital or traditional. From these components, the "CMO as MT" must craft a company and brand-specific marketing process that can translate into the impeccable delivery of the brand experience at every touch point (the many situations and instances where the customer engages some aspect of the brand and company), all the way to the very edges of the corporation.

At the same time, the MT must identify the best technologies to make the brand-building process and its associated tools understandable and available to every practitioner in the enterprise, with a view to making their jobs both more productive and more fulfilling. The CMO, as MT, must cope with technology's timeline, and know when to be on the leading edge and when to be a smart follower.

The CMO and CIO must collaborate on finding ways to apply marketing's best practices in the most effective and efficient manner.

We call it the intersection of marketing IP and marketing IT—the intellectual property that companies employ to build distinctive, sustainable brands, and the information technology they employ to put those tools at the productive disposal of everyone in the corporation. The result is faster and more profitable brand growth, both in cash flows and asset values.

The CMO must drive the goal for successful intersection of IP and IT. The principles in this book provide the knowledge and tools in this process.

THE EMM SOLUTION—END-TO-END CONTENT PLUS END-TO-END TECHNOLOGY

We believe that the solution to drive the much-needed marketing revolution is one that introduces an end-to-end framework for marketing supported by an enterprise-wide technology platform. It is important to think of marketing as a process, and as such it can be enhanced by the application of process improvement techniques that have revolutionized other parts of the organization such as supply chain and finance. Once codified, the marketing processes can be enabled through a collaborative and analytical IT support base. Our aim is to create this overarching process, which has as its goal the enhancement of brand equity. Our system is intended to inform everybody in the organization about how to build brand equity using the best practices that have been proven in enhancing brand equity, and to use the measurement tools that fuel continuous improvement. We use technology to free up marketing professionals from their mundane "fire-fighting" and transactional duties to more creative thinking and high value-added activities.

By structuring the processes and the technology end to end for the explicit purpose of brand equity building, the system focuses the organization to work on priorities that are most critical for increasing shareholder value.

Let's explain how marketing processes and their related best practices content can be developed and embedded into a technology platform for enterprise-wide development.

THE COMPLETE WAY OF BRAND BUILDING

The end-to-end marketing framework focuses on effectively building brands as the engines of long-term growth. The effectiveness of the marketing process in building great brands is the core benefit; the efficiency that comes along with this effectiveness is like icing on the cake.

Figure 2.1 illustrates the interplay of dimensions in our system.

FIGURE 2.1 The complete way of brand building.

The complete way of brand building begins with insights as the foundation, works through long-term brand strategy, creates and executes the short-term plan, and is followed by best practice analytics that will drive the next cycle starting at insights—a closed-loop solution that drives long-term brand growth. The components are:

1. **Insights.** This is a process for systematizing the conversion of the myriad of facts and observations into insights, the profound understanding that leads to a business idea that drives profitable growth. Insights are the lifeblood of a successful marketing program and drive the strategy, planning, and marketing execution of the brand.

2. **Domain strategy.** This is a process to identify the domain: the linked set of customer needs within which the brand exists (e.g., oral care rather than toothbrushes and business solutions rather than computers). It also contains tools to identify the spaces within the domain where the brand can and cannot expand.

3. **Brand equity and LEAP.** This sets the long-term vision for the brand, identifies where its equity is placed currently, and identifies the challenge facing the brand. Brand equity is defined and measured and a long-term equity appreciation plan (LEAP) is created for the development of the brand's equity.

4. **Brand planning.** This is the development of the brand's one-year plan and budgets to meet its immediate financial targets as well as the long-term equity goals. It is a highly collaborative process involving various marketing functions and groups to create an integrated marketing strategy that delivers a 360-degree approach to the consumer/customer.

5. **Brand activation.** This comprises the marketing mix that connects the brand to the customer. It includes product development, advertising, media planning and buying, promotion, direct marketing, interactive, brand touch, PR, and other such processes.

6. **Marketing metrics.** The marketing mix vehicles are supported by a comprehensive metrics structure that links a brand's financial outcomes to the strength of its brand equity. This, in turn, is linked to each of the executional drivers such as communications and innovation.

EMBEDDING THE PROCESSES IN AN ORGANIZATION

Introducing new processes to marketers who are accustomed to ad hoc personal operating styles in a large global organization is a challenge, but our way of building brands can also be exciting and stimulating. The content is very important to the adoption of new processes and it can be structured in a way that makes it user friendly during the execution of the process. Content in the form of digital templates, checklists, score-cards, and tips makes it easy to apply in a day-to-day work environment, as opposed to the tomes of training manuals gathering dust on shelves. Figure 2.2 shows how simple and easy our system is for busy marketing professionals to begin to use immediately.

Another important contributor to the adoption of processes is how the best practices content is delivered to the users. We call this Just-in-Time Expertise (JIT Expertise). This enables the relevant knowledge and best practices to be pushed to a particular user as he is doing a task. Pushing the content dramatically increases the likelihood of its usage during work.

Here is an example. Kimberly-Clark (KC) is transforming its marketing processes from being product-centric to being brand-centric. A groundbreaking team including marketing, IT, and vendors such as SAP are developing a new marketing technology system under the title of *Brand Builder.*

Even though KC brands are among the world's most trusted and valuable, the company realized that merely focusing on product performance functionality could no longer deliver satisfactory results for the shareholder. The transformation to a brand-centric company is redefining the way KC thinks about its consumers, brands, and categories, and about itself as a brand builder.

One of the reasons for undertaking this transformation was shareholder pressure demanding a tighter linkage between the management of brands as assets and the delivery of superior financial return. Jane Boulware, former KC Vice President of Marketing Services, stated it concisely, "You must touch both the head and the heart, and when you do that effectively then you get a higher growth rate and a higher shareholder return."

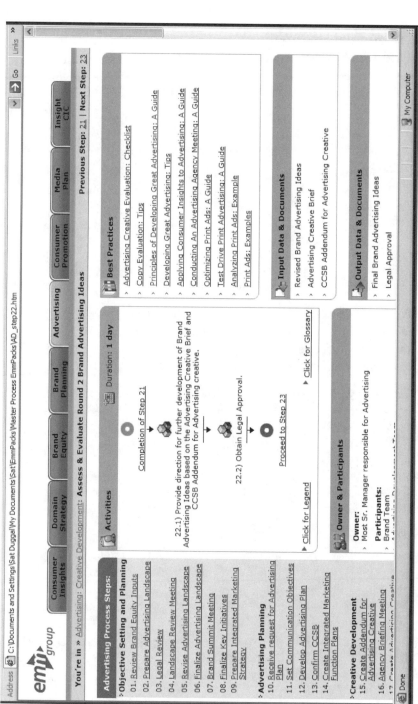

FIGURE 2.2 Marketing process and best practices content delivered for the digital age.

Interview: Jane Boulware
On the Marketing Transformation Process

Our initial goals and steps in our marketing transformation process were as follows:

1. We used EMM Group to help us conduct an audit of our marketing capability, understand what we were good at, and what we needed to improve.
2. We looked both internally and externally for best practice processes.
3. We aimed for excellence, not perfection.
4. Finally, we concluded that we needed to focus on what mattered—finding and owning the high ground.

There are three areas of transformation that the company focused on: process, technology, and organization.

Process. From a process perspective, we were determined to look at it holistically, end-to-end. To do that, we had to map the process of how we do marketing. We integrated and linked the resulting process, and enabled it with technology to create the KC way of brand building.

Technology. Once we developed the processes with EMM Group and others, we partnered with SAP to develop an online tool that we call Brand Builder, which is the one place at every marketer's fingertips that is available 24/7 to deliver best practices, best knowledge, analytics, and a repository of organizational strength.

Organization. Unleashing the full potential of BEM required us to redefine roles, responsibilities, and capabilities of KC marketers.

We have created a center for excellence to manage marketing investments, create process and tools for constant innovation, and build competencies to ensure that the changes that we were making were sustainable and embedded in a learning culture.

We are working together to develop "common where it counts" marketing processes and tools to ensure that everyone has what he needs 24/7 to work at best practice levels wherever he may be in the world. Most importantly, we have rekindled the passion of our marketers by making them accountable for what they love to do—building brands.

This progress at KC verifies the encouraging news that the marketing function can now look forward to robust enterprise systems, combining knowledge, best practices, collaboration, process enablement, on-the-job training, and metrics for continuous improvement.

THE END-TO-END TECHNOLOGY PLATFORM

Technology is a catalyst that can provide data and analytical tools that change the way marketing decisions are taken from purely gut-driven instincts to a more fact-based approach. To do this effectively, the technology platform for marketing should have the following characteristics:

▶ **Meets the effectiveness and efficiency requirements of end-to-end business processes,** with the ability to ultimately meet the functional requirements of all elements of marketing within one solution.

▶ **Uses a single integrated system** that will consolidate the current use of disparate information silos.

▶ **Has an easily configurable user interface** that can provide different interfaces for different constituents, support for multiple end-user operating system platforms, content viewers, and web browsers.

▶ **Offers easy standards-based integration** with added tools within the solution set as well as other enterprise applications.

▶ **Leverages existing IT application platform standards and investments** for both current and planned enterprise software purchases and utilizes in-place procurement and vendor relationships to the fullest extent possible to limit costs.

▶ **Is cost-effective,** to improve company profit margins, return on investment (ROI), total cost of ownership (TCO), and long-term maintenance costs.

Figure 2.3 shows how a prototypical marketing solution stack integrates an end-to-end architecture.

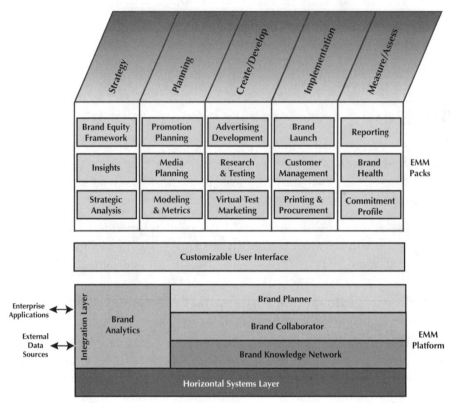

FIGURE 2.3   The marketing solution stack.

The components of the end-to-end solution architecture include a digital asset and document repository that serves as the marketing knowledge center. This invaluable component of the technology solution is explained further in Chapter 11.

Other components of the solution are team collaboration software that enables collaboration among marketing project teams, and planning software that allows the common planning and tracking of all marketing elements such as media, promotion, direct mail campaigns, and others, in one place.

Another important component is the analytical engine that integrates internal and external data and makes it available for metrics tracking and analysis to support the marketing processes. This also enables scenario planning. Such an analytical tool is illustrated in Figure 2.4. Each of these components are explained in further detail in Chapters 10 and 11.

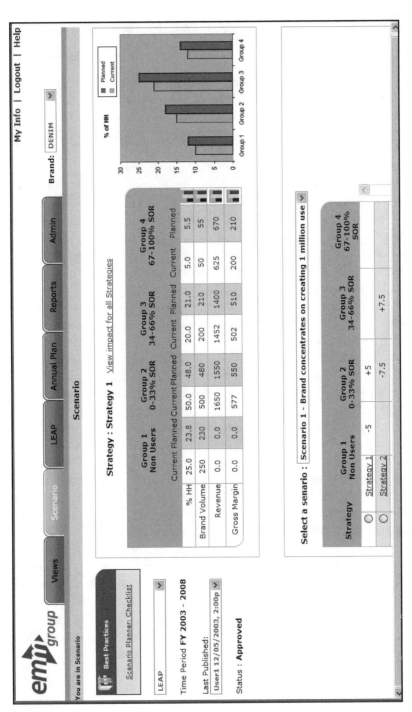

FIGURE 2.4 Example of an analytical tool for scenario planning.

THE "GO-TO" GUY/GAL: MANAGING KNOWLEDGE AND COLLABORATION

In previous eras, there were usually people around the organization (often in supportive staff roles) who knew the brand history, how to get things done, to whom you needed to go for a decision, and other necessities of effectively navigating through the company culture. The corporate hierarchies of reporting charts were usually not very helpful in understanding "how things really get done around here."

With corporate staff cutbacks, those go-to people are long gone. Marketing personnel find themselves in a revolving door or job change and with globalization and increased speed of doing business, the marketing function has become more confusing. So managing knowledge and collaboration has become a new corporate priority for the CMO.

In large organizations, marketing is often practiced very differently in one business unit versus another. Managers moving from one part of the organization to another usually have to learn new ways to do strategy, planning, and execution. Long on-boarding times are the norm. This issue is further exacerbated by the lack of a process or capability to retain knowledge. The lack of an institutional knowledge repository that maintains a brand's history and learning is a debilitating weakness. The results of marketing programs are rarely measured and no mechanisms exist for building a corporate memory of best practices knowledge. When a manager takes up a new responsibility, she gets very little context of what works and what does not. Costly mistakes are often repeated, and painful lessons are thus relearned.

Marketing processes are marked by an unusually high amount of collaboration. Not only do they involve many individuals and groups within the marketing organization, but also personnel from other functions (e.g., finance, sales) as well as across organizations (e.g., agencies). Today's competitive leverage is through creation of global brand franchises. This requires consistency in the brand's strategy and coordination of its execution across geographies. Collaboration at this level, however, can be tedious and time-consuming. Collaborative technologies have made a significant contribution in alleviating similar issues in other functions within organizations, and we are convinced that marketing should take full advantage of these technologies as well.

SUMMARY

The solution to the problems confronting the marketing function is the combination of end-to-end process enabled by technology, and single mindedly focusing on building brand equity. This process/technology combination implies a company-wide adoption of a new way to practice the craft of marketing. The savings in more effective and efficient marketing can be in the many millions of dollars. The increased revenue from enhanced brand equity is almost incalculable.

Marketing leadership must understand how the seamless combination of process and technology transforms how day-to-day marketing tasks get done in a superior manner. The online tools we have illustrated in this chapter demonstrate that situation-savvy technology—pushing the tools onto the desktop to provide easy access to best practices, procedures, and collected knowledge—is a key component to making the future work.

part II

PROCESSES FOR LONG-TERM BRAND BUILDING AND PLANNING

Process-led transformation is the key to unleashing the growth power of marketing. This section provides processes for insight management, brand strategy within a consumer needs space, brand equity management, and long- and short-term planning.

Chapter 3

Insights: The Heart of the Brand

Chapter 4

Domain Strategy: A Powerful Growth Stimulus for Brands in Every Industry

Chapter 5

Building Brand Equity: Brand Vision and Brand Challenge

Chapter 6

Long-Term Equity Plan: Brand Imperatives

chapter **3**

INSIGHTS: THE HEART OF THE BRAND

> ➤ *Do you have an insights-hungry company?*
> ➤ *Do you understand your brand's "Moments of Truth"?*
> ➤ *Is your entire organization focused on developing insights about the brand?*
> ➤ *Do you have a "voice of the customer" to capture what you know about the brand?*
> ➤ *Do you have a process for generating insights from every corporate function?*

IT ALL BEGINS WITH INSIGHTS

We define an *insight* as a profound understanding of the customer and customer needs that leads to a business idea that drives profitable growth. It's significant that the icon for the EMM Way of Brand Building shows insights at the center. That's our way of emphasizing that brand building begins with insights. We believe that the central insight provides the light that allows the marketer to see into the customer's heart. The same insight illuminates every step on the pathway to building a stronger brand.

Marketers' belief in the centrality of insights was not always so intense or widespread. One of the great changes in brand building and business building today is the importance placed on harnessing the power of insights across the entire business value chain.

What is most useful in our approach to insight development is that we do not believe it to be the exclusive province of the intuitive genius or even the market research department. Rather, we believe insight development is a requirement of every professional in the organization and that it is an inherent capability of everyone in the organization. Every marketing leader can turn his or her organization—indeed the entire enterprise—into an insights machine with the right process, the right tools, and the right training. In the same way that marketing and brand building are processes, insights can be generated by a process. Systematized insights generation can become a sustainable competitive advantage.

Interview: Jim Stengel, Global Marketing Officer, Procter & Gamble

The way we do business is not a mystery. But how we execute against it, and the surprising innovation we can bring to the market because of our consumer closeness, will help us to continue to win. We must always remember that the Consumer is Boss and adopt the mentality of permission marketing. Our industry will falter if we aren't focused on consumers first.

Pringles Lunch Box Insight

 Our Pringles brand team identified kids' lunch boxes as a missed opportunity for the brand. Through research we learned the major barrier to trial here was the packaging, which simply contained too many chips for one sitting, and wouldn't fit in a lunch box. The answer was Pringles Snack Stax.

We launched Snack Stax with a relevant message to each of our key audiences: to the parents, we promote the ease of use; to the kids, the excitement of the product; and to our retail partners, the colorful, compact packaging for shelf space.

We have moved a lot of our marketers out into the field to work with Costco, Wal-Mart, and Metro in terms of their brand and how we can build value together. We get involved with deep original research with them. This established a different relationship with the retailer than we have ever had before, one which is based on a co-understanding of the shopper, whom we are both trying to please.

The whole discussion with retailers is based on our shared understanding of what is happening in the store. Our process also revolves around thinking through a deep consumer understanding. Who are the most productive and profitable customers for the future and how do you really touch those consumers?

Prilosec OTC is Holistic Marketing

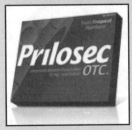

We have stayed ahead of the industry and had impressive growth over the last several years because we have been doing several things right. One example is our market introduction of Prilosec OTC. We began with an understanding of the consumer, very specific targeting, and tremendously penetrating holistic marketing. We penetrated to the influencers through a viral effort to the consumer, and got them genuinely believing in the product. We utilized TV advertising, but TV accounted for a much smaller percentage of that brand's launch efforts than most launches you see today.

Our process revolves around thinking through a deep consumer understanding. Who are the most productive and profitable customers for the future and how do you really touch those consumers? Also, we employ a tremendous retailer tie-in. Prilosec was a grand slam for product launches: we hit a 20 share in just five days! This was in a competitive well-established mature category.

See the Pringles Snack Stax commercial at the book's website, *www.newmarketingmission.com*.

THE MOMENT OF TRUTH

We adhere to the belief that every brand wins the affective commitment and practical purchase loyalty of the customer by developing the insights that allow the brand to own the "moment of truth." For most brands there are actually three moments of truth. First is when the product is in use and the combination of "brand touches" during that usage experience reinforces the customer's loyalty to the brand. P&G has spent millions on product fragrance improvements and packaging improvements on its Folgers brand to own the moment of truth in the early morning coffee experience. No matter what your product or service, no matter whether your buyer is a 12-year-old girl using her first lip gloss or a hard-nosed corporate purchasing manager evaluating building and grounds maintenance, you must deliver during the moment of truth as defined by that buyer.

A second critical moment of truth occurs **_before_** the "moment of truth" represented by the usage experience. It's the few seconds or few minutes just before the purchase when the buyer is considering an array of choices. In the consumer products industry, it's the moment of truth in the aisle at the shelf where the customer passes judgment on the array of benefits, both real and emotional, you are offering him/her. For virtually all consumer package goods brands, this has been the most neglected of the moments of truth. Now major marketers such as P&G are spending millions to capture that moment of truth. Some are delving deeply into exotic fields like "semiotics," the study of symbols and memory, to link the physical package to the range of emotions that trigger a favorable purchase decision. Listen to Jim Stengel's reaction to P&G's research among consumers at the moment of truth at the retail store shelf:

"The direct impact on how we do business differently as a result of this research is the new emphasis on design at P&G. We have a major initiative on building design much earlier into our product development process. We are now focused on the entire brand experience for the consumer. We are bringing designers into our R&D organization; they are working years upstream. We are thinking about product development in a really different way because of a focus on aesthetic and industrial design. This changes the desired qualifications of the people we hire and the dynamics of how we do marketing and product development. This would not have happened or accelerated without an understanding that we have developed through these studies of how a shopper behaves."

A third and in some ways the most elusive of the moments of truth is that one that forms the core of your brand promise. For Kimberly-Clark's Huggies, long-term brand equity is built upon the profound insight that Huggies disposable diapers help to make "happy babies." For Nike that seminal moment of truth is not about shoes, it's about "self realization through exercise." It's about Nike owning that feeling one gets not from winning a race but from doing one's personal best. To its millions of adherents, the Nike swoosh is not about Michael Jordan; rather it's a talismanic symbol that "I care about doing my very best."

Insight development is about the range of moments of truth from the essential insight that drives affective commitment ("happy babies") to the in-store purchase decision to the in-use experience (the big lush sound from the tiny iPod). That's why we say everyone in the company can and should be an "insight detective." That's why we have built a process, and developed a best practice organizational construct enabled with tools to turn your company into an insights-hungry, insights discovery machine.

In later chapters, you will read how the three types of insights discussed above drive the three categories of metrics that build brand equity, specifically "continuous innovation," "communication," and "brand touch." Insights provide a kind of silver thread that ties together the brand equity building process that comprises the EMM Way of Brand Building.

Now that you understand the centrality of insights, let us move to the processes and tools that can transform your company.

Observations and facts tell us *what* customers do—but insights tell us **why** customers behave the way they do

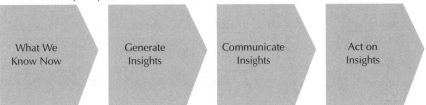

FIGURE 3.1 Insights process: the four major process chunks.

KNOW WHAT YOU KNOW

In our experience all companies have a wealth of knowledge about their business, their customers, and their competitors. Unfortunately, most companies do not know what they know. Their knowledge is scattered about the corporation, much of it secreted away in the fragile memories of current and former employees. Many companies have created whole departments run by specialists in knowledge management to address the challenge of knowing what they know.

The biggest challenges faced by these knowledge management professionals is not managing the "knowledge" that exists or even finding lost data, but gaining agreement on what is truly knowledge and what is merely random data that is actually irrelevant, misleading, or worse still, wrong.

That's why we advocate the creation of a specific repository of brand wisdom. We urge every organization to take the time to create a logical taxonomy of what your company knows about the customers of your brand and the markets in which the brand competes. Our name for this taxonomy is "The Voice of the Customer." See Figure 3.2.

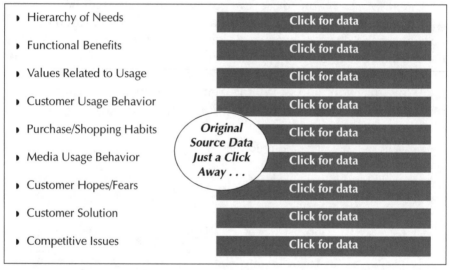

FIGURE 3.2 The Voice of the Customer.

The Voice of the Customer (VOC) arrays the company's knowledge of its customers in a logical manner. As can be seen in Figure 3.2, it encompasses the entire experience of the brand from a list of current insights about the customers' experience with the brand down through actual usage occasions, demographics, media consumption, buying habits, and so on.

One of the interesting components of the Voice of the Customer is the so-called "Customer Solution." What are customers doing today to create a benefit that they cannot obtain from using current products or services in the category? A classic customer solution was consumers' use of baking powder as a dentifrice to produce a better end result (fresher mouth feel and whiter teeth). This customer solution led to the development of various baking powder additives to dentifrice products. In fact, it led to the entire line of Arm and Hammer dentifrices.

Building the VOC is a collegial task requiring the active participation of experienced representatives from many company functions.

The purpose of the initial VOC creation is to achieve three things:

- Agree on what is true, reliable, actionable data: the "basic truths" of the business;
- Agree on what needs to be explored because it is poorly understood;
- Agree on what is totally unknown and needs to be addressed rapidly.

From this initial VOC creation, the business team can begin developing its "learning plan." Learning is one of the three basic obligations of the marketer (the other two being "making the numbers"— succeeding at meeting revenue and margin targets—and building brand equity).

But merely assembling what you know and building a learning plan is not enough. You must be able to build insight creation into the very DNA of the company. You must create a process, an organization, and tools to keep the insights coming.

Let us digress a moment to describe two factors that will make insight discovery a challenge. One is the pride of the internal professionals in your market research function. Many market research departments are notorious for believing that they "own" the insights process, because they understand everything about their customers and product category. They are unprepared emotionally to admit any ignorance because, in effect, doing so indicates that they have failed in their responsibilities to the company.

The second challenge is even more daunting: How do you know what you don't know? The combination of market research hubris and not knowing what you don't know can erect an insurmountable barrier to your insights creation process.

These challenges can be overcome. You can create a process to have every function identify its unknowns. The key to this process is something we call IWIKs ("I wish I knews") and we've built them into our best practice brand-building process through something called "landscapes."

HARNESS THE CREATIVE POWER OF THE ORGANIZATION THROUGH LANDSCAPES

The IWIKs play a seminal role in the process we have devised to identify insights and drive innovation. Many companies, especially in the fashion and cosmetics industries, categorically reject the worth of a process to create insights and transform the insights into innovation. To them, innovation is the private domain of the designated corporate creative genius. They deny the value of a process aimed at harnessing the creative power of the entire organization. We respectfully disagree.

In the brand-building process, you should ask every functional area in the company to look for IWIKs from its unique perspective. Specifically, you should ask for IWIKs as part of the process step of creating what we call *landscapes*. Every function in the company, on an annual basis, produces a *landscape* that outlines what is going on in its specific area of activity, whether that be R&D, media, market research, competitive analysis, packaging, store operations, sales, finance, logistics, or advertising. Each landscape template requires that the function formally identify IWIKs. What is it that you would really like to know in your area?

Our process also encourages _**anyone**_ in the organization at any time to report any fact, occurrence, or observation that seems to suggest an issue worth further investigation or, in other words, is an IWIK. The overall process is geared to address both the regular annually produced IWIKs and the spontaneous IWIKs that sprout from anywhere.

Some people, upon hearing this process of generating numerous IWIKs from all corners of the organization, will have a rather surprising reaction, which is, "What will we do with all the unanswered questions on our limited research budget?" The right response is that every unanswered question is a potential gift. The chance of any given IWIK generating an insight that leads to competitive advantage is quite small. On the other hand, having lots of questions from lots of people from all corners of the organization substantially enhances your chances of generating an insight that can lead to competitive advantage in communication, in product innovation, or in brand touch across the customer brand experience stream. Cast the net wide enough, deep enough, and frequently enough and you have a better chance to catch (or synthesize) "the big insight."

Under ideal circumstances, an organization will produce lots of IWIKs and will have in place the process and the people to winnow out the irrelevant issues and focus on those few insights that can produce advantage.

THE INSIGHTS MANAGER

You can create an organizational construct for doing just that. The insights process should be driven by an organization that recognizes two critical truths: (1) while anyone can produce an IWIK, some people are far better at identifying insights than others; (2) those closest to an individual discipline are generally the best at sorting the wheat from the chaff. Therefore, our process in effect funnels all of the IWIKs through those individuals (we call them "insights managers"). Their immediate task is simple: compare the IWIK to the Voice of the Customer. If that step suggests further review, the insights manager exposes the issue to those people in the organization who have specialized knowledge of the issue in question.

By this simple process, the internal insights manager can rapidly winnow out those issues (IWIKs) of little merit and focus on those that the best minds in the company believe can be developed into a profound understanding. According to Christensen and Raynor, midlevel managers typically play a crucial role in every company's innovation process, as they shepherd partially formed ideas into fully fledged business plans in an effort to win funding from senior management. Their job is to sift the good ideas from the bad and to make good ideas so much better that they readily secure funding from senior management.[1]

A corollary to the rule that some people are better at identifying insights than others is that a stimulating IWIK can come from anyone in the organization or, indeed, any place on the face of the planet. That's why we are so interested in creating a culture of insight consciousness or an insights-hungry organization.

But there's another reason we have designed a process that involves numerous disciplines to identify insights: to maximize the chance that the insight will be turned into something tangible and profitable . . . an innovation.

The process exposes IWIKs to every key function, and thereby enrolls as supporters the very people with the best judgment and most incentive to turn ideas into innovation. The process asks each relevant function to pass the IWIK through a series of screens that can generate metrics for comparing the value of an insight:

> Brand equity alignment or synergy
> Margin implication
> Speed to market
> Effect on volume
> Cost/ROI

Once an IWIK-inspired idea passes an initial screening process, it is re-examined against all items in the portfolio to begin the process of prioritizing its importance in the pipeline.

Let's explore these metrics:

Brand equity alignment or synergy. An idea that does not support or is not consistent with the basic equity of the brand is going to get discarded or passed to a different brand or perhaps to a separate new product process. The fact is that many ideas are brand or domain neutral; there are "good ideas" that can be used by many brands without affecting equity issues. But the very best ideas enhance brand equity—such as a running shoe tread design that allows runners to believe they can run faster when they wear Nikes.

Margin implication. Some IWIKs lead to great insights but productizing the insight costs so much that the product's profit margin would be impaired or its price forced to levels beyond consumer acceptability. In such cases, the process will either discard the idea altogether or recycle it into R&D for the purpose of exploring ways to reduce costs. Plasma screens are a good idea based on the insight that customers will invest in enhancing their home entertainment experience, but their rapid penetration depends on meeting customers' price point expectations.

Speed to market. This is one of the most underappreciated issues in marketing. Studies suggest that the first mover on an idea or technology seizes a disproportionate percentage of available profits. Yet, many companies dawdle over ideas and delay commercialization unconscionably. The purpose of this screen is to identify whether this idea can be commercialized rapidly. This can become an important factor in assessing its competitive value within the brand's overall innovation program. General Motors's commercialization of electric cars could not proceed fast enough, and Toyota and Honda seized the marketplace advantage with the hybrid electric/gas powered cars.

Effect on volume. Initially, this is a ballpark number aimed at placing the insight or innovation into perspective . . . Is this a breakthrough with major volume potential or a "nice-to-have" that will protect share? At a second screening stage, companies apply other methods to calibrate the volume from the idea, but initially they need use only experience and "success models" from similar innovations. For example, Crest's insight about the desirability of a superior low-cost whitening treatment (Whitestrips) added millions of incremental dollars to brand revenue with no cannibalization of the volume of the basic dentifrice brand.

Cost/ROI. A surprising number of insights can be brought to market as innovations without capital investment or with funds that qualify as an ongoing cost of doing business. One good example is innovation in advertising copy brought to the public with funds set aside for new commercial production that year. But many innovations (such as Gillette's wildly successful M3Power razor) do require capital or do incur an ongoing expense. Most companies have adequate evaluation approaches. What they don't have is enough ideas to turn into innovation.

Good news! A true insight often spawns lots of different innovations across the entire brand-building continuum. The Folgers "morning coffee fragrance" insight provides numerous examples of how insight leads to innovation. The story of Folgers' discovery of the importance of the odor of coffee in the morning has been told in other places, especially by Dr. Clothaire Rapaille, a noted consumer researcher who helped P&G unlock the insight regarding the role of fragrance and coffee in the human experience.

Elio Leoni-Sceti, Executive Vice President Category Development, Reckitt Benckiser, explains how Reckitt uses insights to drive product innovation. (See page 102 for an expanded introduction to Reckitt Benckiser's marketing philosophy.) He also discusses the advantage of international branding that leverages the insights through multiple market executions of the success model.

Interview: Elio Leoni-Sceti, Executive VP, Category Development, Reckitt Benckiser

Insights and the Continuous Flow of the Innovation Pipeline

There is no company that can survive with one or two lucky moments. To keep our innovation flow successful, we keep our focus on the search for relevant insights, and we develop products that leverage them to answer real consumer needs. It's like completing a puzzle: the insights are the holes, and products are the pegs; the faster you understand the shape of the hole, and the products that match it, the higher are your chances to be first to launch and win in the market.

Our insights process ensures that we have a visible pipeline with consistent innovation. So, insights generate ideas that are screened and mapped to gaps in product categories. Let's take an example: the toilet bowl cleaners category. And let's simplify by dividing it into two segments: products that you use manually to clean the toilet, and what you put in the toilet for continuous cleaning or freshening the bowl. These two segments are called "manual" and "automatic."

Now, to compete and lead in the toilet bowl category, we need to find the relevant insights that our products can answer, and so satisfy the real underlying consumer needs. Let's take for example the "automatic" segment, where a key insight is that consumers seek for the convenience of an automatic product release, but they fear that—in so doing—they are compromising on the cleaning performance. Then we'll match this insight with the existing product offering, and identify possible gaps. If we find one, we focus R&D to work at a product which fulfills it, and addresses the related underlying consumer need. In this example, it would be a product that is automatically released, but fully delivers on the desired cleaning performance, with a credible reason to believe behind it. Doing this exercise category by category, and segment by segment—with an eye over the next 3–5 years—generates the continuous innovation flow that any successful company needs to achieve, if it wants to remain such in the long term.

The Advantages of International Brands

A brand with truly international scope has a great advantage. Of course, there are efficiencies of scale, such as the typical manufacturing and distribution economies. But more importantly, we have found that our consumer insights—when they are real and relevant ones—are often the same across regions, in most parts of the world. With a sound insights process, you can build around it a proper implementation plan, and a full success model that can be implemented and quickly replicable in new markets. This is a huge advantage in both speed and chances to win in the market. Let's take Vanish, which is a fabric treatment brand. We have a clear understanding of the consumer insight that motivates people to treat their fabrics, and we have a full success model around this, inclusive of product mix, communication strategy, in-store execution plans, etc. When we enter new markets, we have been able to simply apply this model, capturing market leadership within 18 months. That is a key advantage of international branding, which is often overlooked: a proven platform, a success model for new market introductions.

Another advantage is that you have a broader platform for innovation, which also becomes much simpler to build on. If a company focuses on innovation, as we do, the simpler and more consistent the platform of one brand is, the more effective the development work on it is. The reason is simply that the same effort will be applicable to many geographies and products, and does not need to be "tweaked" for each of them. The resources can stay more focused and the results much more effective than if we were developing innovation, let's say, on four smaller platforms.

Dell Computers provides another example of insights driving opportunity.

Case Study: Dell Computers

One of the most important recent insights relates to Dell Computer's discovery of the importance of service. Michael Dell is one of the most successful entrepreneurs in the U.S. and has grown Dell Computers to become one of the world's largest personal computer companies. But Dell once faced a "make or break" company crisis, and quivered on the brink of extinction, because of a massive problem caused by a defective part. Michael Dell realized the threat posed to the survival of his company by this problem and he focused the company onto solving the problem by dramatically increasing his service capability over the telephone. He knew that hundreds, even thousands of people would need a solution to the problem, and so he took as many people as possible and turned them into phone responders. As many people have realized, causing a problem for a consumer also gives one the opportunity to convert them during this "moment of truth" by superior response to the problem. That's what happened to Dell. Consumers, many of whom in the past had problems with other brands of computers only to be frustrated by their attempt to solve that problem, were introduced to a company that had the capability to respond to a problem relatively quickly with live human voices.

For most consumers, Dell's response to the problem was much more reassuring and "brand equity building" than the fact that they had suffered a problem in the first place. Most computer users recognize that all computers have problems, but here at last was a company that made itself available to solve the problems.

It did not take Dell management long to understand that the buzz about their problem was more positive than negative. They decided to dramatically enhance the service capability of the company. The rest is history! Even today, a Dell owner who has had a problem solved by the company's superb service will likely choose to repurchase a Dell computer. There may be comparable, perhaps even better performing, personal computers at a lower price on Internet sites or at a mall electronics store. However, what potential purchasers don't know about brand X is whether anyone will be available to solve their problem. What they do know about Dell is that they are only an 800 number or a mouse click away from help, 24/7.

The power of insight is demonstrated by the fact that, in an industry which prides itself on technological superiority, Dell would be able to separate itself from the competition on the basis of good telephone support with a sympathetic, helpful human voice.

Some insights are so profound, so high on the means–end chain that they can extend their influence to an entire consumer domain—a concept we will develop in the next chapter. These high-level customer insights, because they tend to focus on customers' emotions and needs that are high on the pyramid of affective values, unlock customer permission for the brand to move into areas where it has little or no technological superiority. What the brand does have in these situations is emotional superiority, and the trust of their customers.

OTHER TOOLS OF THE INSIGHT TRADE

We referred above to the spontaneous developments or discoveries that cause someone in the company to send an IWIK to the insight manager, in effect saying, "Here's something interesting that happened in my area of the company that may have implications for the brand. You should look at it." The insight manager has some tools to evaluate this IWIK. Among the very best tools are three:

The Competitive Scenario Tool

In this case, the Insight Manger (IM) creates two teams representing the company and its major competitor. The IM asks the teams to develop a scenario about how each would respond to the new IWIK (it could be a new patent, a new media opportunity, a new packaging material, some new software, etc.). The teams then use their experience with their own company or the competitor to evaluate the importance of the IWIK, how both companies might use it, and the implications for each company's business. The scenario approach was originally developed by Shell Oil in the 1980s and has received significant publicity in major business strategy journals. In our experience, the approach works well in creating and evaluating insights.

The Cross-Trend Analysis

This approach is especially useful when you are seeking insights about opportunities, in other words when you are actively seeking to create an IWIK for evaluation. The essence of this approach is looking for mutually reinforcing synergistic trends that will drive a major business idea. An example will clarify the approach: A major trend recognized by everyone is aging and the need to care for the exploding group called the "old old" (those over 85). A related trend is the geographic dispersal of families such that the younger generation is not physically proximate to provide personal care. A third trend is the dramatic growth in wealthy elderly people who have the financial wherewithal and the desire to provide for their own care. Put these three trends together and one can recognize a huge potential for prepaid "nursing home insurance" sold to the wealthy elderly.

Practitioners of this tool often create a laundry list of trends and direct the business leadership through an exercise that asks, "What does the coalescence of these trends mean for our business today and tomorrow?"

The Looking Backward Story

This approach begins with an IWIK identifying some new development (e.g., a new demographic trend, a new legal or regulatory development, a competitive patent announcement). The IM asks one of the experts in the company to write a story about this development from the perspective of five years hence—"looking backward" at the effect it has had on customers, competitors, and the company. That "looking backward" story then is circulated to interested parties within the company to solicit their insights or recommendations on how the company should respond today.

SUMMARY

Insights build and sustain winning brands. That's why you must create an insights-hungry culture. Insights create advantage across the entire brand-building continuum, from the moment of truth contained in the core insight ("Huggies means happy babies") to the moment of truth across the buyer's desk, to the in-use moment of truth when your product or service is experienced by the customer.

Insights are everybody's business, not the exclusive province of an enlightened few. They can be developed through a metrics-driven process supported by an organization trained to use a few valuable tools.

One of the foundational tools is the Voice of the Customer, wherein the company archives the accepted truths across a range of behaviors and attitudes relevant to the customer. The VOC is the first step toward turning your company into an insights machine that can dominate its domain.

ENDNOTES

1. Clayton M. Christensen and Michael E. Raynor, *The Innovator's Solution: Creating and Sustaining Successful Growth*, Boston: Harvard Business School Press, 2003, p. 10.

chapter 4

DOMAIN STRATEGY: A POWERFUL GROWTH STIMULUS FOR BRANDS IN EVERY INDUSTRY

➤ *How can you achieve greater leverage from the time and dollars you have invested in your brand(s)?*

➤ *How can you extend your brand franchise to higher growth and new categories?*

➤ *How can you achieve 2× your current growth rates?*

The purpose of marketing is to generate growth. The vehicle to do so is the brand. Some skeptics say that the days of brands are over. Perceptive observers, on the other hand, see a number of major branded businesses achieving high growth rates, even from brands that are old and may at one time have been flat or dormant. Dove from Unilever is an excellent example. In 10 years, it has grown from $250 million in annual sales to $3 billion in annual sales, and continues to grow. Over the period 1998–2002, Dove's average annual revenue growth rate was 27 percent.

Dell has been able to expand far beyond its origins as a low-price desktop computer company. It has done so successfully in both business-to-business (B2B) and business-to-consumer (B2C) segments. In B2B, the Dell brand has expanded into laptops, printers, network equipment, and services. In B2C, Dell has expanded into PDAs, home wireless network systems, and recently, home entertainment. Soon, consumers will need a system integrator for the home and it's a good bet they'll turn to Dell.

For a long period of time, Dell sustained an annual revenue growth rate of 30 percent per year.

The Virgin brand is possibly the best example of the most value creation from imaginative brand leverage. Virgin has successfully entered global businesses as diverse as music retailing, air travel, train travel, insurance, and wireless telephone service by identifying and nurturing the silver thread of "Virgin-ness" in each of those markets.

All these brands and several more vibrantly growing ones that we have studied, employ a process that we call Domain Strategy. This is the strategy to generate growth by making a brand more relevant to more people in more parts of their lives. It is the most powerful growth weapon in the business arsenal.

Before we discuss this powerful new strategic tool, it is instructive to trace the origins of the skeptics' view of the demise of brands.

THE CURRENT STATE OF BRANDS

From their beginnings, brands have been conceived as a strategy for building share in a category. Tide was a brand in the detergent category, Oldsmobile was a brand in the automobile category, Oscar Mayer was a brand in the prepared meats category, Sun was a brand in the server category. These brands strove to compete for customer spending in their categories. Although the business model was successful for some brands for a long time, three major problems emerged:

1. If the brand competed in a low-growth category, it became hard to achieve above-category growth. While innovation could create temporary advantage, it could quickly be matched, and might start a costly innovation and spending war.

2. Because the brands viewed themselves as performance-driven, they spent heavily on performance improvement, but found that the business benefit of each subsequent improvement quickly approached zero. The return on performance improvement investments declined. The result of the performance improvement race was that the brands became function and attribute driven. Teams of engineers and scientists thought up new attributes or new ways to deliver speed, power, and efficacy. As we shall see, functional attributes occupy a low rung on the brand-building value chain.

3. As this performance sclerosis was developing, the cost and complexity of marketing was accelerating. The amount of television advertising GRPs (gross rating points) that one Tide washload or one Oldsmobile automobile or one Oscar Mayer wiener generates has halved over the past 10 years. The number of 30-second commercial spots required to reach 65 percent of the target population in four weeks for most major brands has gone up from 10 to over 100 over the same period because of the disintegration of the network monolith. The number of media choices—network TV, cable TV, print, outdoor, stadium signage, Internet—and channels has exploded. The cost of salesforces has escalated remorselessly. There is no sustainable business model for a slow-growth brand in a slow-growth category to carry the burden of this media inflation, channel proliferation, and sales cost escalation.

THE BREAKOUT STRATEGY

The new brand-led growth solution requires new thinking by the brand owners themselves because their customers (we'll use that word to signify the consumers targeted by B2C brands and the customers targeted by B2B brands) have been looking at things in a different way from brand owners for a long time. Brand owners have to break out of their self-imposed limitations to catch up with customers. We offer domain strategy as the process for doing just that.

Customers Think in Terms of Needs

Customers seldom think in terms of product or service categories. They think in terms of their needs. As customers or business people or end users, their lives are an amalgam of needs to be met and solutions to meet them. The customer of a cosmetics brand isn't consuming in the cosmetics category, she is meeting a need for confidence and self-esteem based on the way she feels about her appearance and how others perceive her. The business customers of a computer technology brand are not consuming in that category, they are meeting a need to feel confident about their efficient and competitive business performance. The consumers of health care products are meeting a need to feel reassured that they are addressing and managing their condition in an optimal way. Customers think not only in terms of functional needs, but specifically in terms of emotional needs. They want to feel confident, self-actualized, a sense of achievement, and to live a life of harmony that's secure, happy, and fulfilled. Thus marketing works best when it appeals to values at the pinnacle of the "pyramid of life." Successfully doing so leads to higher financial returns for the firm.

Hierarchy of Customer Needs

An easy way to visualize customer needs is to think of them as a pyramid with an ascending hierarchy of importance from lowest to highest. Figure 4.1 illustrates what we mean.

At the base of the pyramid are the "price of entry" needs. These represent the minimum the customer expects from any product or service in a category where she is considering a purchase. These needs are functional—customers want the product or service to work, to do what it says it does.

Ascending the hierarchy, the customer will have some functional needs that, once the price of entry needs are met, represent a higher level of potential satisfaction, to be met by superior performance over and above basic functionality. The needs are still functional, but somewhat refined.

Ascending the hierarchy still further, the customer will have some emotional needs that are of a higher order entirely from functional needs. In the cosmetics example that we cited earlier, it is easy to see that the functional performance of creams, powders, and lotions escalates to emotional fulfillment for consumers—making them feel good about the way they look, an important component of self-esteem. It is just as easy to think about the emotional needs associated with purchasing and driving an automobile. It is perhaps not so easy to think about the emotional needs driving the selection of a desktop computer. Until, that is, you think about the passion that Apple users have for their Macs and the pride in practicality of Dell users, and their confidence in the service support that they know stands behind their machines. The same escalation to emotional benefits applies to customers selecting business products and solutions—they're looking for a sense of achievement, pride, and accomplishment in their selection, and its effect on business results.

At the very top of the hierarchy is the highest-level need that you can strive to fulfill for a customer. In the academic literature, these are called "terminal" values, and they include needs such as family security, social recognition, and freedom. They are needs beyond which there is no further upward escalation. It's not always possible to attain these high values in marketing a product or service, but the great brands aim as high as they can possibly reach.

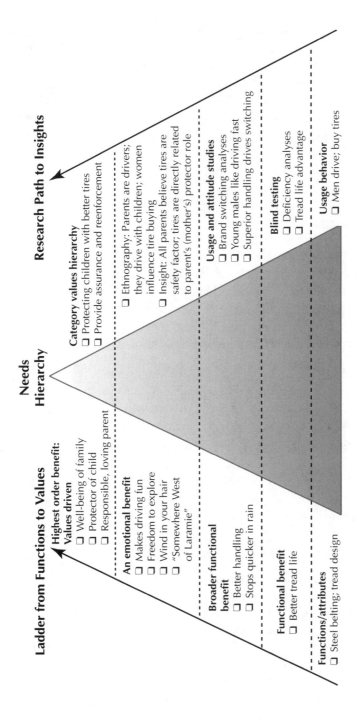

FIGURE 4.1 Hierarchy of needs for a brand of tires.

Figure 4.1 illustrates how a brand of tires may climb the hierarchy of values. The base level is functional. The tires must work to support another activity, driving. Over time, the functionality can be raised, so that tread life is extended and performance is improved. However, the customer engagement is still in the area of functional needs. As customer knowledge and insights improve, a certain amount of refinement enters into customer understanding. Behavioral and demographic segments emerge, such as younger drivers, fast drivers, and drivers who treat their car as an object of pride and self-expression.

Deeper digging using techniques such as ethnography (where researchers accompany customers to observe them in their daily lives) reveals new insights. Drivers are not just drivers, but parents; they care for their children and hope to keep them safe at all times. Tires are in the domain of expressing love via family safety and protection. At this stage we are approaching the apex of the insights process and the brand equity pyramid. We have identified what the sociologists call a "terminal value"—i.e., you can go no higher than family love, safety, and protection on the scale of human values. Now the task is to capture that via brand promise and brand touch (the purchase, usage, and ownership experience).

This same hierarchy applies just as well to B2B brands. Buyers and decision makers are not just functional role players; they are human agents with values and emotions. They work for a sense of accomplishment, to achieve great things, to feel a sense of pride and worth, as well as to contribute to the realization of their company's inspiring mission statement. These and many other emotional values are integrated into their decision making and their relationship with your brand of technology or office supplies or financial services. The hierarchy of needs is equally as applicable as an insights device in B2B and B2C.

Needs Are Not Bounded by Categories

The types of needs customers feel are not bound by any construct as limiting as product or service categories. If customers seek fulfillment in the cleanliness, hygiene, orderliness, and attractiveness of their bathroom, they are not thinking about the toilet tissue category and the facial tissue category and the towel category and the soap category and the bathroom appliance category and the bathroom furniture category and the bathroom fixture category. They are thinking about the feeling they have when they enter their bathroom—about its compliance with their core values, about its reflection on them, about how it looks to guests, and about the total bathroom experience. The same is true of customers of baby care, business services, transportation, health care, and telecommunications. Customers link a broad set of needs together into a solution set that addresses their highest-level needs. Needs are linked across these solution spaces; they are not discrete.

Brands Can Address a Linked Set of Needs

If you define your brands in a fashion that's bounded by category limits, then you are not in tune with your customers, and you are missing significant potential for growth. Customers link a set of needs in their mind, and have demonstrated willingness to buy a single brand to meet all these linked needs. That's why Dove can successfully sell soap, skin cleansers, deodorant, shampoo, moisturizing cream, and toner to women who feel that the health of their skin is important to their feelings of self-esteem.

Similarly, Dell is able to sell a wide range of products, peripherals, and services to customers whose need is for reliable technology solutions that are easy to understand, easy to use, easy to own, and easy to buy. All in all, buying, owning, and using reliable technology that gets the job done is "as easy as Dell." This is one of the great advertising summations of a domain strategy promise, but the key to Dell's success is relevance of the promise across a wide range of customer needs and the quality of the delivery of the promise, not the advertising. Figure 4.2 illustrates the multiple dimensions Dell now has consumer credibility in which to compete.

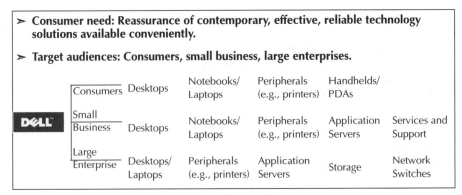

➤ Consumer need: Reassurance of contemporary, effective, reliable technology solutions available conveniently.

➤ Target audiences: Consumers, small business, large enterprises.

DELL					
Consumers	Desktops	Notebooks/ Laptops	Peripherals (e.g., printers)	Handhelds/ PDAs	
Small Business	Desktops	Notebooks/ Laptops	Peripherals (e.g., printers)	Application Servers	Services and Support
Large Enterprise	Desktops/ Laptops	Peripherals (e.g., printers)	Application Servers	Storage	Network Switches

FIGURE 4.2 The Dell brand has stretched on multiple dimensions.

Dove and Dell have increased their product scope within defined needs of skin health (Dove) and reliable technology solutions (Dell). Virgin tackles the concept of linked needs differently. For this brand, the common need state is the feeling many of us share of being helpless (and helplessly ripped off) in the face of the giant bureaucratic corporation. This can be defined by customer complaints such as, "We can't get through to a human on the phone, we can't get an answer to our questions, we can't get restitution for a product or service that fails, we get overcharged, we are refused accommodation to our time needs or convenience needs—and we get frustrated." Virgin takes the role of the consumer advocate for every man, offering more respect, more flexibility, better service, and a more human face. The shared need is to be treated with respect and responsiveness, whether it be in telephony or insurance or music sales. Meeting this need cheerfully and consistently is the "silver thread" of Virgin-ness that runs through all the seemingly disparate businesses in the Virgin portfolio. It is a service-centered positioning, as depicted in Figure 4.3.

Virgin, having started out in the music industry, then leveraged some of its brand's strategic drivers—exhibited by the associations of irreverence, individualism, and being iconoclastic—to help it deepen its presence in the travel industry, as well as expand into mobile phones, online auto sales, and insurance.

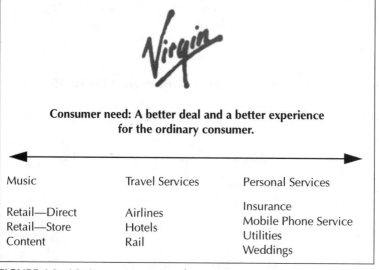

FIGURE 4.3   Virgin: service-centered positioning.

Many factors play into a brand's ability to cross a broad domain of customer needs. The reality is that it is the brands that have built the strongest credibility, making the most of their strategic drivers, that have been most successful with product and market extensions.

IDENTIFYING STRATEGIC BRAND DRIVERS

The challenge marketers face is in identifying the key dimensions of brand equity, profiling their brand against these dimensions, and then modeling core strategic brand drivers. But the profiling process must be moved beyond an expansive cataloguing of a brand's associations. The focus must shift to those that have real impact and then draw conclusions between strategic brand drivers and business outcomes. This enables both the tangible and the higher-order intangible associations with the brand to be better leveraged and managed.

For example, suppose an up-and-coming brand in a competitive segment in the soft drink industry spends millions each year in support of its brand. It recognizes the need to grow the business, but wants to make sure that the nature of the support it is giving the brand is measured and strategic so that the foundation for future growth would be solid rather than haphazardly built. It wants a better understanding of the consumer "levers" to pull.

A more in-depth brand equity profile and model would help this business better understand how the brand is perceived and what aspects of the brand were most compelling in encouraging customer loyalty and a willingness to pay more (i.e., allowing the brand to command price premiums).

The first step in the process is building the model around which the brand equity is based. Its foundation is the product or service, which is described for its attributes (not its or the brand's benefits), scope, uses, and where it is acquired, used, or seen. Building on that foundation are the four key dimensions of brand equity:

1. The brand reputation, the tangible and intangible perceptions of what it is "good at."

2. The values and personality of the brand and its users, providing insight into the brand's "character."

3. The multidimensional benefits delivered by the brand—functional, emotional, and self-expressive.

4. The areas of brand leadership, along with perceptions of its momentum in the market and ability to persuade stakeholders that it is relevant.

Businesses that intend to reap the benefits of using brands as a driver of business success need to begin the process of identifying and managing, in a systematic and structured way, the associations that contribute to brand equity and that are critical to enhancing the brand's value and the extent to which it financially impacts on the business. This activity is domain strategy.

HOW TO DEVELOP YOUR DOMAIN STRATEGY

Like everything else in marketing, domain strategy is a process. It is a process that you can apply to your brand or your business. Here's how.

1. Listen to the customer.

An important aspect of domain strategy is the understanding that the customer defines the domain. This is key to the breakout strategy. According to Jim Stengel, global marketing officer at P&G, "We must know the consumer, before we can know how to market to that person. . . . And we must make that attachment/connection (to the consumer) rationally and emotionally and we cannot just pay lip service to this."

We simply need to listen to the customers describe their needs and all the needs that are linked together in a single need space, in order to begin to define a domain in which our brand or business can grow. There are some structured research techniques available to do this, as we'll see, but the fundamental principle is to let the customer, not the brand, define the domain.

2. Find the highest-level, overarching need.

The needs in the domain are linked because they all contribute to a single, overarching need that the customer is pursuing.

The theory behind this idea is an analysis of customer behavior called a "means–end chain." All customers have certain values by which they live their lives. Their "end" is to achieve these values. Values include states such as "a comfortable life," "inner harmony," "self-esteem," and "safety and security."

When choosing products, customers identify and select those products whose "means" result in "consequences" that contribute toward the consumers achieving their end of attaining a particular value that's important to them. Dove brand has the means (moisturizers and other ingredients) that have desirable consequences (softer, healthier skin), which help consumers to achieve their end of the self-esteem that results from confidence in their femininity.

For customers of Dell, the overarching need may be the sense of accomplishment they feel as a result of mastering the world of technology and identifying reliable, easy-to-use, easy-to-buy, and easy-to-own solutions to generate personal or business productivity. This need will be felt by a segment of the customer population that is probably not in the earliest adopter group, and favors reliability over cutting-edge innovation and being on the frontiers of performance. It is also not for the group that wants the absolute lowest price for a personal computer or technology components. There will always be a less expensive alternative. Dell has been able to retain leadership with a good price/value perception without having to match every price competitor. Charles Schwab has done the same in the discount brokerage and financial services categories. For customers of Virgin, the highest-level need is the self-respect of negotiating a good deal from a customer advocate and avoiding the sense of exploitation or disadvantage experienced with other brands.

3. Identify the subsidiary need spaces in the domain.

Once the high-level need is identified, and the broad outlines of the domain are in sight, the brand owner can seek to identify all the subsidiary need spaces in the domain. This is the process that took Dove from a brand of bar soap to a system of skin care that covers numerous product categories from cleansing to moisturizing to toning, and embraces soap, deodorant, shampoo, exfoliating lotion, moisturizing lotion, creams, and toner. Consumer needs differ at different times of the day, so Dove offers both day creams and night creams.

Olay is expanding in a similar domain, and has gone one interesting step further. This brand has found a holistic beauty need among women that includes both inner and outer beauty. As the brand's first entry into the world of "inner beauty," Olay has introduced a line of vitamins that contribute toward skin and hair health. These vitamins underline their role as a beauty treatment with the same "cosmetics-quality" package designs and styles as the Olay brand creams and lotions. If Olay is successful, what other inner beauty needs can they meet, such as relaxation therapy (via spa treatments, for example), or stress reduction (yoga courses)?

Refer to the product line of Olay at the book's website, *www.newmarketingmission.com*.

The subsidiary need spaces are dynamic, and can change over time, even though the overarching need does not change. Dell can migrate from meeting the needs for personal productivity to meeting the needs for digital entertainment networks and products. It is still operating in the domain of confidence in reliable, easy-to-use, easy-to-buy, and easy-to-own technology solutions.

4. Draw a domain map and size up the business opportunity.

It is useful to capture the domain strategy concept in a graphic called a domain map, as illustrated in Figure 4.4.

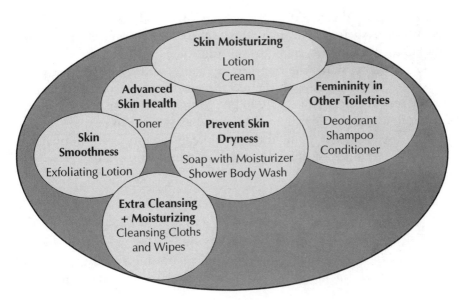

FIGURE 4-4 Dove domain: restoring femininity.

In this conceptual map, the need spaces are identified as skin moisturizing, advanced skin health, skin smoothness, and so on. These are not product categories; they are consumer needs. As the process advances, the total domain size can be identified, the total growth rate (made up of the weighted average growth rates of each of the spaces) can be estimated, and the business potential of the domain can be sized up.

This is achieved by identifying how much customers spend on solutions in each space. The sum and the trend can be quickly ascertained from primary and secondary data sources. The domain map becomes an expression of the business potential for the brand to grow. When the Crest brand expanded its domain from cavity prevention to oral-centered self-confidence, it expanded the size of the space in which it competes by over four times and the growth rate of the businesses in its portfolio by over six times.

5. Formalize the growth strategy.

The final step at this stage is to formalize the growth strategy. The opportunities within the domain can be evaluated using scorecard techniques. Scorecard metrics include opportunity rankings (the size and growth rate of the spaces, the opportunity for margin, the degree of contest anticipated, the quality of the brand fit) and cost of seizing the opportunities (such as investment costs, costs of entry, and degree of difficulty in identifying new advantaged solutions).

Having scorecarded the opportunity, it's time to go to the board or the executive committee with the recommendation to grow the brand in the domain. The opportunity should be dramatic in terms of new spaces to enter, new growth rates, and new global expansion routes.

With this new playing field the brand can identify new pathways to growth. When done successfully, such brand expansions can have several advantages:

- Distributors may perceive there is less risk with a new product if it carries a familiar brand name. If a new food product carries the Heinz brand, it is likely that customers will buy it.

- Customers will associate the quality of the established brand name with the new product. They will be more likely to trust the new product.

- The new product will attract customer awareness quicker, along with a greater willingness to try or sample the product.

- Promotional launch costs (particularly advertising) are likely to be substantially lower.

So, a domain strategy has five component parts:

1. Listening to the customer
2. Finding the highest-level, overarching need
3. Identifying the subsidiary need spaces in the domain
4. Drawing a domain map and sizing up the business opportunity
5. Formalizing the growth strategy

Case Study: P&G's Domain of Self-Esteem Through Beautiful Skin

Domain strategy can accommodate multiple brands from a single brand-owner's portfolio. P&G SK-II is a brand success story, and the global domain strategy work of which SK-II is a part also helps to support Max Factor and Olay brands.

With justifiable pride, P&G management refers to the success story of its new product SK-II (SK is an acronym for Secret Key) in the skin care category. SK-II illustrates P&G's domain-based approach to brand development. Here are several outstanding factors for this extraordinary marketing success story:

1. SK-II is a beauty skin care system that retails in the U.S. for $130. It provides a high-status, high-priced brand with a price point that is beyond P&G's traditional mainstream products groups.

2. It was developed based on careful customer research and understanding of customer need at a very high level in the hierarchy of needs—the desire for the self-esteem that comes from keeping skin young and beautiful. This high-level need became the defining need for the domain in which SK-II brand was developed.

3. SK-II was globally developed and first introduced in Japan, where women represent the most demanding consumer group in the world for cosmetics and beauty products. Once SK-II succeeded in Japan, it was introduced successfully in world markets.

4. P&G scale was leveraged to introduce a product globally in a category that P&G is not known for and in outlets such as specialty department stores outside of P&G's traditional channels. It expanded P&G's distinctive competence to include individual beauty consultants in kiosks. This is an example of how successful domain development work can raise profitability by introducing new price points into the brand portfolio. (P&G executed a similar strategy with Crest Whitestrips, which was introduced at a $40+ price point, representing real value for the consumer because the alternative source was in the professional channel at 10 to 20 times that price.)

5. The same technology that supported SK-II was also used for introductions of new products in the brand portfolios for Max Factor and Olay. By being able to integrate technological breakthroughs on multiple global product platforms, P&G can leverage and optimize similar innovations in the same domain on different brands to multiply its growth opportunities.

Also extraordinary is how SK-II illustrates integrated marketing in product development, consumer knowledge, and marketing mix (including package and product design). Here is an excerpt from the Harvard Business School Case study authored in 2003 by Professor Christopher Bartlett, P&G Japan: The SK-II Globalization Project (refer to the Internet site to order the case from Harvard Business School, *www.harvardbusinessonline.hbsp.harvard.edu*).

"This global product development process was set in motion when consumer researchers found that despite regional differences there was a world-wide opportunity in facial cleansing. The research showed that, although U.S. women were satisfied with the clean feeling they got using bar soaps, it left their skin tight and dry; in Europe, women applied a cleansing milk with a cotton pad that left their skin moisturized and conditioned but not as clean as they wanted; and in Japan, the habit of using foaming facial cleansers left women satisfied with skin conditioning but not with moisturizing. Globally, however, the unmet need was to achieve soft, moisturized, clean-feeling skin, and herein the GBU (Global Business Unit, under the direction of A.G. Lafley, future CEO of P&G) saw the product opportunity—and the technological challenge.

A technology team was assembled at an R&D facility in Cincinnati, drawing upon the most qualified technologists from its P&G labs world-wide. For example, because the average Japanese woman spent 4.5 minutes on her face-cleansing regime compared with 1.7 minutes for the typical American woman, Japanese technologists were sought for their refined expertise in the cleansing processes and their particular understanding of how to develop a product with the rich creamy lather.

Working with a woven substrate technology developed by P&G's paper business, the core technology team found that a 10-micron fiber, when woven into a mesh, was effective in trapping dirt and impurities. By impregnating this substrate with a dry-sprayed formula of cleaners and moisturizers activated at different times in the cleaning process, team members felt they could develop a disposable cleansing cloth that would respond to the identified consumer need. After this technology "chassis" had been developed, a technology team in Japan adapted it to allow the cloth to be impregnated with a different cleanser formulation that included the SK-II ingredient, Pitera.

A U.S.-based marketing team took the task of developing the Olay version. Identifying its consumers' view of a multi-step salon facial as the ultimate cleansing experience, this team came up with the concept of one-step routine that offered the benefits of cleansing, conditioning, and toning—"just like a daily facial." Meanwhile, another team had the same assignment in Japan, which became the lead market for the SK-II version. Because women already had a five-or six-step cleansing routine, the SK-II version was positioned not as a "daily facial" but as a "foaming massage cloth" that built on the ritual experience of increasing skin circulation through a massage while boosting skin clarity due to the microfibers' ability to clean pores and trap dirt.

Because of the premium pricing strategy, the SK-II Foaming Massage Cloth was packaged in a more elegant dispensing box and was priced at $50, compared to $7 for the Olay Facial Cloth in the U.S. And Japan assigned several technologists to the task of developing detailed product performance data that Japanese beauty magazines required for the much more scientific product reviews they published compared to their Western counterparts. In the end, each market ended up with a distinct product built on a common technology platform. Marketing expertise was also shared—the Japanese performance analysis and data were widely used in Europe, for example—allowing the organization to leverage its local learning."

In the end, P&G built upon the SK-II success in Japan to launch a global product.

Summary

Marketing has transitioned from being product-centric to being brand-centric. This enables the brand management group to break out of low-growth or mature product categories. The domain strategy model provides a process for any brand to map its opportunities and by listening to the consumer, to find new innovative products and even create new categories that will be accepted by a loyal consumer base.

chapter **5**

BUILDING BRAND EQUITY: BRAND VISION AND BRAND CHALLENGE

➤ *What is brand equity and how does it improve financial results?*

➤ *How can your brand grow at faster than category rates?*

➤ *How do you prioritize brand investment?*

➤ *Do you have a clear vision for the next five years?*

➤ *How can you identify a vision that will both inspire and direct your global organization?*

➤ *What are the challenges for achieving your brand vision?*

We have identified the critical insights process on which to base a differentiated delivery of solutions to customer needs, and we have defined and sized a domain where sustainable high levels of growth can be engineered.

The next step is to create the brand equity framework with a brand vision, brand challenge, and a long-term equity appreciation plan (LEAP).

Figure 5.1 illustrates where the brand equity framework lies in the EMM Way of Brand Building.

Building brand equity is a difficult task *but it's not the arbitrary, ad hoc, mysterious black magic that creative marketing geniuses want us to believe that only they can master.* With discipline, care, knowledge, and, most important, process, brand equity can be built systematically over time.

FIGURE 5.1 Brand equity and LEAP.

In order to make this complex process simpler, we've established three tools that guide the brand equity management process:

1. *Brand vision* is a composite document describing where the brand aspires to be, both as a business and in customers' perceptions, and the core assets it will employ to get there.

2. *Brand challenge* is an honest appraisal of the barriers to overcome to get there.

3. *LEAP* is the five-year plan to achieve the vision and meet the challenge.

WHAT IS BRAND EQUITY?

You can pose two simple questions to understand brand vision and brand challenge:

1. What is brand equity?

2. How does it drive financial results?

In the financial world the word "equity" is used to refer to financial instruments that represent an ownership interest in the financial outcomes of a company or investment. A representation of how a number of equities are performing as a group is often expressed as an index number—the Dow Jones Industrial Average, the S&P 500 Index, the Nasdaq 100, and so on. When that number goes up, the financial outcomes of the companies whose equities make up the index have improved.

Brand equity refers to that element of a brand's perception that directly determines the financial outcomes of brand ownership. When the brand equity index goes up, the financial outcomes of the brand (top-line revenue growth, gross margin, and brand value added) will go up.

Brand equity can be described as the perceptions that consumers have of a brand at any point in time based on everything they have seen, heard, or experienced.

Also see *BrandEquity.htm,* a desktop shot of our guide for understanding the definition and importance of Brand Equity at the book's website, *www.newmarketingmission.com.*

THE POWER OF PERCEPTION

Many CFOs have an initial negative reaction to the idea that a perception—an intangible and primarily emotional feeling in a customer's mind—can determine a financial result. However, if you multiply feelings about a brand by millions of consumers, you can create financial outcomes. The reputation of a company is often based on emotional foundations such as trust and familiarity. During the recession of 2001–2003 we witnessed that when the company's reputation sinks—often as a result of emotional reactions—shareholder value is immediately damaged.

Consider the University of Michigan Consumer Confidence Index. It is derived entirely from an emotional reaction—the answer to this question: How do you feel about the economy and how it will perform in the future? It frequently varies as respondent confidence see-saws between optimism and pessimism. The researchers massage these emotional responses into an index number and publish it each month. If perceived consumer confidence goes up, the stock market usually reacts positively and shareholder value is created, and if consumer confidence declines, billions of dollars of shareholder value can be destroyed in seconds.

So, we can easily see how emotions, perceptions, and opinions have an immediate effect on value creation and financial outcomes.

BRAND PERCEPTION IS BUILT UPON MULTIPLE TOUCH POINTS

Outside observers often make the mistake of equating marketing and the brand-building process exclusively with communications, and specifically advertising. They think that marketing is the end of the value chain, the last "coat of polish" to a business proposition that is already formed. But if we define brand perception as everything customers see, hear, and experience, we quickly realize that marketing encompasses the company's entire business proposition. In the best brand-building companies, "everyone does marketing." Anything and anyone who touches the customer is marketing to that customer. Hence the growing attention to the concept of a brand's "touch points."

The customer's experiences include the quality of the product or service, the efficiency of delivery and the supply chain behind it, and the responsiveness of the sales representative and the call-center operator. Customers do not depend solely on advertising to experience the brand. They can tell if the company listens to its customers or not. They see the company's trucks on the road, the décor of its offices and branches, the messages and visuals on point-of-sale material, and the content of direct mail and email messages, just as much as they see advertising or packaging. Think of United Parcel Service (UPS), Federal Express, or Southwest Airlines as exemplars of brand building in every contact point with consumers.

HOW DOES BRAND EQUITY DRIVE FINANCIAL RESULTS?

Brand equity is a perception that can translate into commitment to a brand. There are two kinds of commitment: attitudinal and behavioral. Attitudinal commitment is a feeling about a brand that can be thought of as a continuum. One well-known version of this continuum uses a "4 A's" mnemonic:

Unaware. I have no feelings about the brand because I haven't heard about it.

Aware. I've heard of it but am not sufficiently persuaded by anything I have seen or heard to buy it.

Accept. I have heard of the brand and I accept it as qualified to be in my brand set and I buy it occasionally.

Adopt. My experience of this brand has made me adopt it and I buy it quite regularly.

Adore. This is my brand of choice for the needs it meets; I buy it on every possible occasion, in fact I would go out of my way to buy it and avoid situations where it is not available. I recommend it to others.

As customers ascend this continuum, their improving attitudinal commitment turns into behavioral commitment:

▶ This brand is responsive to my needs.

▶ I have confidence that it will always meet my needs.

▶ I have trust and respect for all the brand's offerings.

Therefore, behaviorally:

▶ I make repeat purchases to enjoy the relationship I have with the brand.

▶ I make a point of belonging to a community of brand users who are smart enough and like-minded enough to share their loyalty to the brand.

▶ I am ready to recommend the brand to others.

▶ I am willing to pay a premium for the brand because I experience not only better value but also the emotional rewards of loyalty.

▶ I am confident about trying any new offerings the brand might present to me from time to time.

As a result of these increasing commitments, customers will try a brand, or continue to buy a brand (i.e., exhibit brand loyalty), and allocate a brand a greater share of their expenditures in any given category.

And if they truly love the brand, they will be more likely to try anything new within a brand's domain that it introduces to the marketplace. Figure 5.2 details the process and metrics that can measure the power of brand commitment.

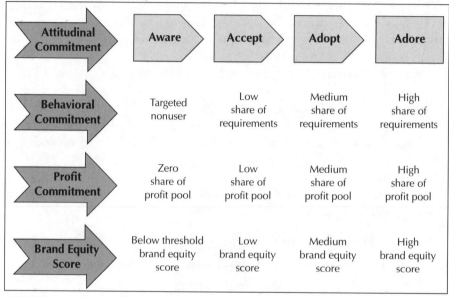

Attitudinal Commitment	Aware	Accept	Adopt	Adore
Behavioral Commitment	Targeted nonuser	Low share of requirements	Medium share of requirements	High share of requirements
Profit Commitment	Zero share of profit pool	Low share of profit pool	Medium share of profit pool	High share of profit pool
Brand Equity Score	Below threshold brand equity score	Low brand equity score	Medium brand equity score	High brand equity score

FIGURE 5.2 The power of brand commitment.

Brand equity is associated with high brand loyalty. High loyalty is associated with high margins. If you have my loyalty, you do not have to give your product away and you do not have to reduce its price, so you can increase your effective brand margin; you do not have to promote as much, people come to the store or the website and will choose your brand anyway. So, brand loyalty can be measured by repeat purchase or share of requirements. These are good metrics for measuring brand loyalty.

Brand equity can also close a credibility gap for product performance and reliability. Customers will pay more for the risk relief and confidence they get from known and trusted brands. Christensen and Raynor[1] describe this, "When customers aren't yet certain whether a product's performance will be satisfactory, a well-crafted brand can step in and close some of the gap between what customers need and what they fear they might get if they buy the product from a supplier of unknown reputation. The role of a good brand in closing this gap is apparent in the price premium that branded products are able to command in some situations."

For example, even if Heinz ketchup costs marginally more than another brand, a loyal consumer will still buy Heinz. This is because Heinz has created an expectation and a standard taste that meets that consumer's needs, which says that "this tastes good," "I know its good," "it makes me think of hamburgers," and the consumer is willing to pay a premium price for Heinz, which implies high brand equity, high brand loyalty, and very high margins. Therefore, making customers more committed through stronger brands leads to higher levels of revenue growth, cash flow, and profitability.

For B2B brands, the equivalent of the 4 A's continuum is termed "affective commitment." While B2B customers will probably not tell you that they adore your brand, they show the same low, medium, and high levels of commitment. If they have the fullest level of trust in the brand and have had a long-term, positive experience with it, they will show the same commitment to allocate the fullest possible share of dollars they spend in the space to the brand, they will be less focused on list price and more on the total solution the brand delivers, they will be more open to trying new products and services the brand brings them, and they will recommend the brand to others (sometimes even in testimonial advertisements!). Customers at the top of the commitment continuum will generate high revenue growth and high margins.

Note that affective commitment is a lot different from customer satisfaction. The latter is a snapshot, a moment in time; it provides a satisfactory answer to the question, "What have you done for me lately?" Affective commitment has a projection of future loyalty and future cash flows that customer satisfaction lacks.

WHY BRAND EQUITY IS THE FINANCIER'S DREAM

According to Doyle,[2] "the present value of a brand's future cash flow is a function of four factors: the level of its cash flow, the speed it comes in, the duration it lasts, and the risk of these future returns." Figure 5.3 illustrates these principles.

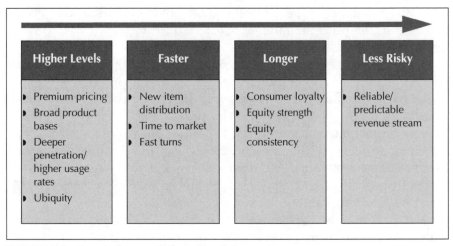

FIGURE 5.3 Brands drive cash flow growth four ways.

Among consumers who have a weak brand perception, the brand will achieve little penetration or loyalty. Where brand perception is strong, the brand will achieve increasing loyalty, with a consequent increase in the level, speed, duration, and reliability of cash flow and revenue. It is the task of marketing—specifically, brand building—to increase the quality of perception among more and more customers.

The challenge in building brand equity is to increase variables such as the affective commitment and the behavioral commitment to the brand. In order to start on the journey to building brand equity, every brand should have a brand vision, a brand challenge, and a LEAP.

BRAND VISION

Brand vision is an expansive, ambitious statement of what the brand could be and where you could take it. Determining the brand vision is the first step in the brand equity framework process, which is presented in Figure 5.4.

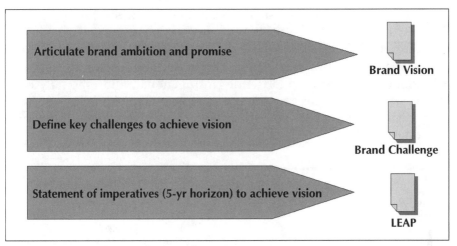

FIGURE 5.4   Brand equity framework process.

The brand vision is the long-term goal we set for the brand. It is a stretching, deliberately ambitious goal that sets the direction for the brand over the next three to five years. Usually, the vision describes the ownership of a desired high-level emotional benefit or equity that a brand seeks to own outright (versus competitors). The brand vision process is depicted in Figure 5.5.

If you've conducted a domain strategy exercise and mapped the domain and its boundaries, you know that you can take the brand beyond its current category boundaries. You may even believe you can be the first to see the potential in the domain and that your brand can "own" the delivery of the high-level benefit that defines the domain. Or you may simply see pathways to growth that weren't obvious before the domain strategy was developed.

Creating the brand vision is an iterative process. It starts by identifying the consumer-defined emotional space described in the doman strategy process.

Once that space is identified, the marketer must create the hierarchy of customer needs relevant to the space. These needs start with the prosaic "price of entry" functional benefits ("the tires fit my car and roll smoothly") to the highest "terminal" value ("the tires keep my children safe and fulfill my responsibility as a parent").

Then the marketers must create an equity map of current brands. What spaces (benefits) do they own? How secure is their ownership of a specific benefit?

This allows the marketer to create an initial opportunity statement describing the brand's opportunities in functional, and especially emotional, terms. From this opportunity statement evolves the Brand Vision Statement, a comprehensive but concise one-page document comprising 10 components. See Figure 5.5.

Component	How It Is Used
Brand Ambition	Desired state—what the brand can become
Rationale	Why we believe BV is desirable/achievable AND the customer-centric/business metrics that demonstrate the rationale for achieving the Brand Ambition
Key Customer Insights	The new/revised customer and brand insights that have helped us redefine our brand vision
Future/New Brand Promise	A simple statement of what our brand will promise to customers in terms of highest-level, emotional benefits
Rational/Functional Support for Brand Promise	Support for Brand Promise from the functional, performance, product, and technology basis of the brand
Brand Essence	Brief statement—developed via the Brand Essence process—of the core essence of the brand
Target Audience	Key audience descriptors, extending beyond verticals to their consumers' attitudinal and psychographic segmentation information
Desired Relationship with Customers	How we will seek to connect with our customers in the future—their expectations, motivations, and drivers
Competitive Environment/ Context	Articulation of other competitive brands in the space, including their vision, and/or expected competitive reaction/intentions
Executional Properties	Key brand properties that may evolve or need to be considered as we scope out new opportunities; includes Brand Architecture

FIGURE 5.5   Brand vision statement.

Even stalled or declining brands can find growth in a well-defined, high-growth domain. Crest brand from Procter & Gamble is a good example. Competing head-to-head in the low-growth dentifrice category, Crest had lost market leadership and was hard-pressed to make headway against its well-marketed and well-entrenched competitor. When it redefined its domain as oral-centered self-confidence rather than toothpaste, several growth accelerators kicked in. Crest was now operating in a market space four times bigger than the toothpaste category, with six times the growth rate. There were category places where it could be first to innovate, rather than cannibalize and compete head-to-head with Colgate toothpaste in a feature and promotion war.

Crest's brand vision could now extend beyond efficacy in promoting healthy teeth, and embrace leadership in delivering oral-centered self-confidence to consumers. This space included beauty (as in a beautiful smile), breath freshness, and gum health. The range of solutions went far beyond toothpaste—to whitening treatments, breath freshening, floss, germ killing, innovative toothbrushes, and many more.

THE HIGHEST NEED LEVEL THE BRAND CAN MEET

Domain strategy releases brand vision from category-bound and product-bound thinking, and refocuses it on consumer needs-based thinking. As we saw in Chapter 4, once the domain has been identified, we can construct a consumer hierarchy of needs for the primary consumer needs uncovered in the domain. The hierarchy of needs is Maslovian—it is based on the premise that, having met their needs on one level, consumers continually strive to ascend to a higher level of need and to meet those higher-level needs. Classically, the hierarchy has functional needs at the bottom, and progressively more complex needs—for safety, belonging, love, and esteem—are ranked progressively higher. At the very top are the highest needs, for self-actualization and spiritual improvement.

If consumers link these highest need states together under a single overarching need state, then they will be very likely to accept one brand that can deliver them all. A bold brand can be very ambitious in this situation.

See our *BrandVisionCompletion.htm*, a desktop shot of valuable tips and reminders to consider when completing the brand vision process; *BrandVisionCompletion.doc*, a checklist of information for developing the brand vision statement; and *OCSBHierarchyOfNeeds.htm*, a hypothetical example of the needs of oral care users for a fictitious brand OCSB, as represented by the Hierarchy of Needs, at the book's website, *www.newmarketingmission.com*.

The Dell brand can embrace a vision of being the number one brand that consumers turn to for reliable, easy-to-buy, easy-to-use, and easy-to-own digital solutions for the home. This space can embrace TV, digital cameras, home entertainment of all kinds, and the network integration and services that make it all work. Microsoft, Sony, HP, and several more brands have sought out ascendancy in this space. But Dell can legitimately have the ambition to win. Why? Because they understand the consumer need ("Confidence in reliable technology that's easy") better than any other brand, and they are trusted to deliver it. They've earned that trust by delivering reliable technology solutions and making them easy in a number of adjacent spaces.

The brand vision should be a comprehensive document that sets out the *brand ambition* (where will this brand be in five years time), and the brand promise and rationale for the promise. This is quite close to a positioning statement—the *brand promise* is the single benefit that the brand will deliver to the customer in order to attract more users and generate increasing loyalty. This promise is invariably an *emotional* benefit. It doesn't matter whether your brand is operating in a B2B space or a B2C space, or even if it seems to be focused on the most functional and operational characteristics. Customers don't just buy products and functionality. They don't even just buy reliability (keeping the promise). They buy relationships, and relationships are based on emotions—trust, confidence, and a feeling of comfort at minimum; sometimes escalating to a feeling of exhilaration (you can get pretty excited about installing a Cisco network!) or a sense of accomplishment (think of the procurement officers at hospitals who purchase supplies and are part of the mission of bringing superior health care and improved patient outcomes to the community; they have a high level of emotional motivation in everything they do).

Scientists and researchers can feel a sense of partnership with the testing instruments from their supplier Agilent Technologies. That is why the Agilent Technologies positioning statement "Dreams Made Real" affirms a powerful affective connection with the customer who is dedicated to discovery. The Agilent Technologies connection to the feeling of discovery for the betterment of humanity transcends product function and price.

The rationale for the promise is the reason the customer should enter into this relationship with a desire to realize the end benefit. The rationale can include functional reasons—for example, "our product is so well made that you can trust its reliability." But it must also have an emotional reason—for example, "our company is so committed to your winning that you'll feel like you have an army of energetic support behind you."

Dell's rational support of its promise of reliable technology that's easy to buy, easy to use, and easy to own includes its world-leading supply chain, its web-based ordering and tracking interface, and its incredibly sound levels of service. But there is a further reason that customers trust and even love Dell. They feel that Dell has a level of understanding and sympathy for them in their use of technology that no one else has. Compare the service you get from Dell with that of any other technology supplier with a web or telephone interface—satellite TV, your wireless or wireline telephony supplier, any of them. You will consistently conclude that Dell has more feeling and more empathy for the customer.

The task of the brand vision is to capture both the rational and emotional support for the brand promise, not only as accurately as possible, but in a way that both reflects and drives the culture of the brand and makes it credible and deliverable. In the new world of brand-led growth, it is critical to unleash the brand-building power that's inherent in every employee.

Everybody does brand building in the winning company of the future. To do so effectively, everyone must live the promise and be part of its rationale. The brand vision is both the blueprint and the code of conduct for the brand-building team.

BRAND CHALLENGE: BRIDGING VISION WITH CURRENT REALITY

In creating a brand vision, there is freedom—and indeed necessity—to be expansive and ambitious. We must stretch to know what is possible, and it requires unconstrained thinking to do so.

The next step is to be candid and objective. Can the brand realistically achieve the vision? If so, what are the barriers and obstacles that must be overcome? This is the brand challenge.

▶ Articulating the gap between the brand vision and the current state enables us to understand the task at hand; is this a major restage of the brand or simply a communications tweaking?

▶ Articulating the current gap with reference to the brand commitment continuum enables us to apply metrics to the gap, and to monitor each year (or any other time period) our progress in closing the gap or meeting the challenge.

In addition to the brand vision, the brand challenge phase requires:

▶ *The brand health summary*, which defines the current standing of the brand with the target audience as measured by sales, consumption, and brand equity scores.

▶ *The brand commitment profile*, which measures consumers' behavioral loyalty to the brand.

See the Brand Commitment Profile at the book's website, *www.newmarketingmission.com*.

The following British Airways example illustrates all of these concepts and explains brand challenge.

Case Study: British Airways

In the early 1980s, British Airways was fighting its "BA—Bloody Awful" image as a government-owned entity. Lord King, the newly appointed chairman of British Airways, drove a management and organizational shake-up during that period and hired a new CEO in Colin Marshall, the ex-GM of the Avis rental car company's European division. Marshall's obsessively customer-centric approach resulted in a radical (for BA) brand vision—to bring enjoyment to air travel through excellence in service—a vision reflected in the "World's Favourite Airline" campaign.

In 1982, BA had a long way to go to being the "world's favourite airline." *The brand challenge was immense.* If they had conducted a brand health monitor, they would undoubtedly have discovered competitively poor ratings on key measures such as differentiation, relevance, esteem, and knowledge, and certainly the brand vision of owning enjoyment in air travel through excellence in service would have seemed an impossible target.

However, Marshall set out to identify the gaps, that in addition to poor financial results included, for example:

▶ **Consumer expectations.** Delivering enjoyment in air travel through excellence in service would require BA to thoroughly, radically change consumer touch points, most of which are listed below. Essentially, consumers expected a very different airline from the then-current state.

▶ **Product.** BA offered point-to-point air travel worldwide, but did not offer the convenience of easy transfer on/off other partner or feeder airlines. Routes were flown with military efficiency, based on efficient utilization of capital rather than for customer needs. The vast majority of equipment used on the routes tended to be older, cramped, vintage 1960s aircraft, unpopular with passengers.

▶ **Pricing.** Notwithstanding customer service issues, BA pricing, though on a par with other "flag carrier" European airlines, did not offer the value, especially on short-haul domestic and European routes, that would deliver against the vision.

▶ **Customer service/culture.** BA staff was notoriously unhelpful, with a history of labor problems—the opposite of "excellence in service."

▶ **Communication.** BA's vintage 1970s campaign "Fly the Flag" did not convey a passion for flying, a dedication to service that the brand vision suggested.

▶ **Packaging.** BA's aircraft livery, logos, and uniforms were rooted in the past.

And if BA had expressed their customer profile in a brand commitment model they would probably have found a relatively high share of requirements among business users (whose options were other state-owned airlines), so there was high behavioral loyalty, but low attitudinal loyalty. Leisure users (with more charter airline choices) would most likely have been located to the left on the brand commitment continuum—low SOR (share of requirements) and low loyalty (behavioral and attitudinal).

This, then, was how the brand challenge that British Airways faced in 1982 might have been expressed.

The objective definition of the brand challenge should be addressed in two ways: words and numbers. In words, the brand challenge should clearly set out the tasks to be accomplished. Examples include:

▶ Increase penetration among small businesses of $50 million to $250 million in revenues, from 5 percent to 45 percent.

▶ Increase the share of requirements the brand commands among the top 1,000 customer targets from 17 percent to 24 percent.

▶ Increase the brand gross margin by 2.5 percentage points by increasing it 0.5 percentage points each year for five years.

Brands too seldom describe their targets with such clarity. The benefit of doing so is that it forces the brand owner and brand manager to confront reality: Can these goals realistically be achieved? Are there any historical parallels that suggest that the achievement is feasible? Are there any marketing strategies that suggest the likelihood of success?

Senior management might well be reviewing many brand challenge documents, either from many different brands if they are managing a multibrand business, or from many different business units that are applying a monobrand in multiple categories. By reviewing these brand challenge documents side by side, they can make decisions about the relative likelihood of success of the various options in front of them, and allocate resources appropriately.

The brand challenge in numbers is an unvarnished set of data indicating where the brand is now, where it needs to be in the future, and the annual milestones to get there in a five-year period. For example, if the brand commitment profile suggests that it will be necessary to both double penetration and double the number of customers in the highest affinity quadrant, while maintaining the current share of requirements commanded by each affinity segment, the brand challenge might look like this:

	Unpenetrated	"Accept"	"Adopt"	"Adore"
Year 0 (Today)	50%	20%	20%	10%
Year 1	45%	21%	22%	12%
Year 2	40%	22%	24%	14%
Year 3	35%	23%	26%	16%
Year 4	30%	24%	28%	18%
Year 5	25%	25%	30%	20%

The brand challenge in numbers provides yearly milestones to check progress, and becomes the basis for the five-year targets in the long-term equity appreciation plan (LEAP), which we will discuss in the following chapter.

Similar brand challenge numbers can be generated for the brand equity score necessary to drive an increase in penetration and loyalty, as well as for targets in revenue growth and brand gross margin growth that result from the overall improvement in brand equity.

 See the book's website, *www.newmarketingmission.com*, for more information on the work plan (brand commitment planner) with examples of this type of brand challenge numerics.

SUMMARY

Building brand equity provides financial advantage for higher, faster, longer-lasting, and more secure cash flows. This is the core task for marketing. Creating the processes for brand vision and understanding the gaps to close in achieving universal customer belief in that vision—through the brand challenge—are key to expanding growth both in scope of products in more profitable new categories as well as improving profits for existing product offerings. This process requires a long-term commitment to equity appreciation.

ENDNOTES

1. Clayton M. Christensen and Michael E. Raynor, *The Innovator's Solution: Creating and Sustaining Successful Growth*, Boston: Harvard Business School Press, 2003, p. 163.

2. Peter Doyle, "Shareholder-Value-Based Brand Strategies," *Brand Management* Vol. 9, No. 1, pp. 20–30, September, 2001.

chapter **6**

LONG-TERM EQUITY PLAN: BRAND IMPERATIVES

> ➤ *Do you know where this brand will be in five years' time?*
> ➤ *Do you know what revenue and profit growth it will deliver?*
> ➤ *Do you know how much that will cost?*
> ➤ *Do you know the five main focus areas on which you must deliver to realize the goals?*
> ➤ *Have you identified the right metrics to measure equity appreciation?*

So, now you have identified the brand vision and the brand challenge for your company or brand. How do you convert these into an actionable plan for building brand equity?

The process for moving forward requires a long-term equity appreciation plan (LEAP). The LEAP provides the five-year plan to bridge the gap between the brand challenge and the brand vision. Figure 6.1 describes how the LEAP is formulated.

As Figure 6.2 illustrates, the LEAP process itself consists of three phases: developing five-year targets, developing the LEAP, and conducting annual reviews to monitor and refine the LEAP.

The three major components:

Brand Vision		Brand Challenge		Brand LEAP
Clear articulation of our brand ambition and promise	▶	Deep understanding of the key challenges we have in achieving our vision	▶	Clear statement of five-year imperatives and roadmap to achieve our vision
Where *can* we go?		Where *should* we go?		How will we get there; are we getting there?
▸ Customer-led ▸ Lofty, expansive goals ▸ Rationalized, grounded in customer insights, data, and research		▸ Where are we now? ▸ What challenges must we meet to bridge the gap or break down the barriers?		▸ Five-year targets ▸ Focused imperatives ▸ Metrics ▸ Progress monitoring

FIGURE 6.1 The LEAP process.

Develop Five-Year Targets	Develop LEAP	Annual Review
Brand equity scores ▸ Brand ownership ▸ Category specific ▸ General BCC profile* ▸ Penetration ▸ SOR/loyalty Net revenue Brand gross profit	Brand vision Target audience evolution Brand positioning Future brand equity scores ▸ Five-year transition Future BCC profile* ▸ Five-year transition 5–6 LEAP imperatives Product/category roadmap Competitive environment Learning plan (IWIK)	

* BCC: Brand Commitment Continuum, discussed in Chapter 9, "Marketing Metrics: Brand Equity Is Money".

FIGURE 6.2 The LEAP process phases.

The key components of LEAP are as follows:

The Five-Year Targets for the Brand. The brand creates two types of targets. Attitude (equity) targets and behavior (purchase) targets. The attitude or equity targets are measured by a series of metrics that capture consumer perceptions across the full range of the consumer experience. The behavior targets are expressed in terms of market penetration (the percentage of consumers using your brand) and the revenue or purchase volume per customer (often expressed as "behavioral loyalty"). Let us discuss each of these in more detail.

1. **Equity goals.** Equity measures the attitudes that drive revenue and growth via the brand equity monitor (discussed in Chapter 9). There are three types of brand equity scores, and the coefficients of each one as a driver of brand revenue growth will be developed over time based on business results. The LEAP articulates three sets of brand equities:

   a. Desired equity ownership unique to your brand—The single high-level equity we desire to own (e.g., for Dell: "Confidence in reliable technology that's easy to buy, easy to use, and easy to own").

   b. Category-specific drivers that define what it takes to win in the category—Those equities that we know drive preference and purchase intent within our category; an example could be safety, style, or performance in Volvo's car category.

   c. General equity drivers that determine the strength and stature of any brand—Usually differentiation, relevance, esteem, knowledge.

Over time, we seek to build a direct link between the brand equity scores and the brand revenue outcomes, in the form of a coefficient or a correlation factor. Progress against the five-year brand targets can be tracked through the brand equity monitor.

2. **Customer behavior goals.** The brand equity goals measure attitudes. The LEAP needs to measure behaviors because behaviors translate directly into revenues. We advocate measuring three simple metrics: (1) the percentage of the marketplace that has purchased your brand at least once in a relevant time period, (2) the number of times they have purchased your brand during that

time, and (3) your brand's percentage of total revenue spent in the space. As we discuss elsewhere, almost any marketing problem can be addressed by understanding these three simple metrics.

A five-year LEAP can be qualitatively and quantitatively depicted as the progress of a consumer along a "brand commitment continuum," in which nontriers become occasional triers and current triers give a greater and greater percentage of their total category needs to your brand. Understanding who these customers are, and how to move them up that continuum is at the heart of marketing and LEAP development.

Table 6.1 on the following two pages provides an example of the goal-setting template for brand equity and for the penetration and loyalty metrics.

Once the goals are set, the next step is the creation of what we call *imperatives*—the major strategies required to bridge the gap between vision and challenge.

WHAT ARE BRAND IMPERATIVES?

In this component of LEAP, you determine the key strategies on which to focus over the coming five years to progress toward your brand vision. We call these major strategies *imperatives*. Others may call them expressions of strategic intent. The LEAP document outlines these imperatives and the high-level description of the projects that will be pursued to deliver on each imperative.

Let us use Folgers coffee to illustrate the concept of brand imperatives. From an intensive analysis of coffee drinking habits, P&G knew that coffee had been losing both household penetration and share of consumer daily fluid intake (share of gallons drunk per day per person) for nearly 40 years. The only usage occasion showing any vitality in the 1990s (the pre-Starbucks period) was the morning occasion. Therefore, Folgers identified a strategic imperative of "Owning the morning coffee drinking occasion."

Additional research, some of it driven by the highly creative concepts developed by Dr. Clothaire Rapaille, identified the deep emotional importance of the coffee fragrance especially in the morning. From this, Folgers developed another imperative: "Deliver a superior coffee fragrance experience."

TABLE 6.1 Goal-Setting Template for Brand Equity, and Penetration and Loyalty Metrics

Brand Long-Term Equity Appreciation Plan

Brand Vision:

Brand Revenue Goals

		Year 1	Year 2	Year 3	Year 4	Year 5
Topline Revenue	$M					
Increase versus YA	%					
Brand Profit	$M					
Increase versus YA	%					

Loyalty Ladder Profile

	Beginning					Ending				
	Group 0	Group 1	Group 2	Group 3	Group 4	Group 0 (Year 1)	Group 1 (Year 2)	Group 2 (Year 3)	Group 3 (Year 4)	Group 4 (Year 5)
% HH	20.0%	33.0%	20.0%	15.0%	12.0%	10.0%	25.0%	25.0%	20.0%	20.0%
% Brand Users	N/A	41.3%	25.0%	18.8%	15.0%		27.8%	27.8%	22.2%	22.2%
% Brand Revenue	N/A	8.1%	18.8%	28.1%	45.0%		2.8%	13.9%	27.8%	55.6%
% Brand Profit	N/A	0.0%	15.0%	31.0%	54.0%		-2.0%	12.0%	30.0%	60.0%
Brand Units / HH										
Price Paid / Unit										
Gross Margin										
Marketing Cost										
Brand Profit / HH										
Total Brand Revenue										
Total Brand Profit										

(continued)

TABLE 6.1 Goal-Setting Template for Brand Equity, and Penetration and Loyalty Metrics (Continued)

Brand Equity Scorecard										
	Beginning					Ending				
	All HH	Nonuser HH	Group 1+ Group 2	Group 3	Group 4	All HH	Nonuser HH	Group 1+ Group 2	Group 3	Group 4
Equity Ownership: Makes Life Better										
Your Brand %	+25%	+7%	+25%	+33%	+37%	+50%	+15%	+50%	+60%	+70%
Competitor A %	+7%	+7%	+13%	+7%	+7%	+7%	+7%	+13%	+7%	+7%
Difference	–18%	+0%	–12%	–26%	–30%	–43%	–8%	–37%	–53%	–63%
General Equity Drivers										
Different/Unique										
Relevance										
Esteem										
Loyalty Score										
Value Score										
Image Score										
Category-Specific Equity Drivers										
1										
2										
3										
4										
5										

Other analysis showed that high-consumption coffee drinkers purchased larger size containers and that brand loyalty was higher among those buying coffee in larger containers. Further detailed research revealed that the "brand" loyalty of large-size container purchases was often loyalty to a size and not a brand. Therefore P&G developed another imperative: "Dominate the large-size container segment of the category."

Note that each of these imperatives can be measured on a scale such as the brand commitment continuum.

IMPERATIVES DRIVE INITIATIVES

Imperatives express a specific strategic intent the brand must realize to close the gap between brand vision and brand challenge over the long term (five years). Initiatives are the programs to turn the strategic intent of the imperatives into marketplace reality. Let's use the Folgers example to explain the imperative/initiative relationship.

The first imperative was "own the morning coffee drinking occasion." The advertising initiative with the brand promise of "the best part of waking up is Folgers in your cup" is the perfect expression of the strategic intent embodied in the imperative. Additionally, Folgers developed a media plan including morning drive-time radio that reinforced the relationship between morning coffee and Folgers. Particularly impactful was the radio mnemonic of the bubbling coffee pot along with the brand promise. We're sure P&G is working on a way to make the coffee odor come through the radio dial!

Because the next imperative was "deliver a superior coffee fragrance," P&G tackled this imperative with two different initiatives, both relating to the bloom or rush of fragrance at the moment of truth when the container is opened. The first initiative involved the heightening of the fragrance at the factory via various technical means; the second involved a new lid closure device aimed at preserving flavor after the container had been opened in the home.

The last imperative was "dominate the large-size container segment." This required a series of initiatives including re-sizing the container, repricing the container, and skewing promotional support more toward the larger size. A critical component of this imperative was enlisting the support of Wal-Mart to embrace large-size Folgers as a key component of Wal-Mart's strategy to increase share of the food business overall via their supercenter format.

The synergistic interaction of these three imperatives has had a dramatic effect on consumers' perceptions of the Folgers brand. It's no wonder Folgers has recently seen its share lead over Maxwell House brand increase to more than 15 share points.

LEAP is deliberately designed to provide the metrics framework for defining and tracking success—identifying the equities we wish to own, and the specific measurements that are our year-by-year goals. We map imperatives from Year 1 to Year 5 in order to set the vision and expectations for the key initiatives that each imperative will generate over time. Each initiative in turn is linked to an aspect of the metrics it is supposed to drive; in Folgers case, these were

- Survey score for "The best coffee to drink when you wake up in the morning"
- Survey score for "The coffee with the best fragrance"
- Measure of coffee penetration and loyalty in heavy consuming households
- Share of the large-size container market

Elio Leoni-Sceti, Executive Vice President, Category Development, Reckitt Benckiser, explained how his company uses a LEAP strategy and a metrics framework.

Interview: Elio Leoni-Sceti, Executive VP, Category Development, Reckitt Benckiser

Reckitt Benckiser is a household products company that has been extraordinarily successful in growing brand equity and brand profitability in relatively unfashionable categories such as household cleaners, fabric treatment or air fresheners. The company not only has a formidable record in brand-led growth, but also led the world in linking brand equity to earnings growth and stockholder value creation. They call their model the Virtuous Cycle (VC). In this model, the company targets a rate of innovation (such as "40 percent of sales revenue from product innovations launched in the last 3 years"), and commits that each innovation will deliver higher brand gross margin than volume it replaces. They set a target for margin growth (e.g., 50 basis points per year), and they set a guideline for the use of incremental margin (e.g., a part to profits, and a part invested in brand equity strengthening activities).

There are four questions they use to validate and keep the Virtuous Cycle virtuous:[a]

1. Why portfolio focus?
2. Is innovation sustainable?
3. How far should we grow investment?
4. Will gross margin expansion continue?

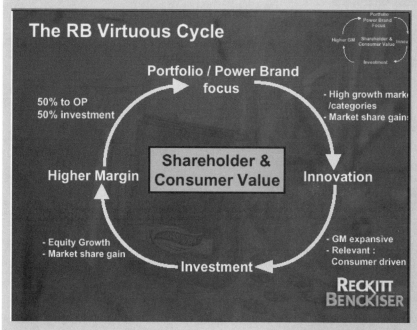

FIGURE 6.3 The Virtuous Cycle used by Reckitt Benckiser.

Why Portfolio Focus?

VC is distinguished by the coherence, consistency, focus, and commitment to translate the strategy into actions at all levels in the organization—across regions and categories.

This model helps us to focus our efforts and fund the investments in our "best brands" for continuous, profitable long-term growth. The "best brands," which we call Power Brands, are those in which we have the most solid competencies, with a leading position, globally, and that compete in the faster growing categories in our markets.

a.   These questions are answered in following parts of this chapter as they relate to components of EMM Group's LEAP module.

In this context a key operating philosophy is: *We do not spend the money that we don't make!* We always want to make sure that the cycle stays virtuous. Do not invest more in the brand if the margins are not expanding to generate the cash to do that. Monitor, evaluate, and revise this annually.

How Far Should We Grow Investment?

As a company we believe investment in brand equity will return longer-term benefits. But, how much and which brands (and how long)?

How much? Brand equity is measurable and actionable on a market or regional basis (such as France, Italy, the United States) but not on a global basis. We measure brand equity with systematic and standardized form on a rolling basis for key markets in key categories. We set goals: For instance, we want to have "intent of next purchase" go from X percent to Y percent, and achieve these goals over three years. We choose to invest in brands to achieve stated goals, and often we choose a category that relies upon consumer pull, rather than categories that rely more on trade push. We believe that the consumer is the boss, and we focus heavily to understand her insights and needs, so we choose to compete in categories in which consumer preference is more important. We see a clear link between the quality of the investments behind the brand and its success, so we focus on quality. By quality we mean advertising in which the unique qualities of the brand are the focus, and which builds consumer preference overtime.

But we like to see short-term evidence as well, and need to reconfirm brand performance year by year. In the majority of cases, if the innovation is relevant, a fast sales response is visible . . . these are the easy ones! More thought needs to be put in when the long term becomes a leap of faith, as no sales response is visible in the very short term. This is when management must make a call about the value of pure brand equity appreciation, and what will this be returning in the long term. Projecting forward, we believe three years is a reasonable (long-term) timeframe for that.

TYPES OF IMPERATIVES

Imperatives are typically few in number—no more than five or six. Their purpose is to concentrate effort, resources, and development on the few strategies that truly matter in achieving the brand's targets. The actual imperatives can vary by brand and business situation, but essentially there are five common types of imperative:

1. Brand commitment profile enhancement
2. Advancing into new domain spaces
3. New product, service, or solution development and innovation
4. Communication
5. Channel management

Other imperatives might include refinements in marketing mix, investment mix, or line extension development.

Let's examine in greater detail each of the five priority imperatives we propose you consider:

Brand commitment profile enhancement. The goal of making the brand more relevant to more people in more parts of their lives is monetized via new penetration and higher loyalty (i.e., a higher share of the customer's requirements devoted to your brand). Customer loyalty and usage rates are the engines of unit, revenue, and profit growth as defined by behavioral brand commitment. You must have an understanding of the specifics of your brand's growth model and be able to focus on the development of a marketing plan and set of tactics geared to that model. The Folgers example above is a classic of brand commitment profile enhancement.

Advancing into new domain spaces. The strategic execution of the brand-led growth imperative (i.e., that brands grow by becoming more relevant to more people in more parts of their business or personal lives) is domain strategy, as reviewed in Chapter 4. The examples we've used include Dove advancing into new spaces in the domain of women's self-esteem through healthy, young-looking skin and Dell's advancing into new spaces in the domain of confidence in reliable technology that's easy to buy, easy to use, and easy to own. One LEAP imperative will include the elevation of growth targets via advancement of the brand into these new spaces.

New product, service, or solution development and innovation. The second most important influence on brand equity and brand perception is a positive brand experience. This is delivered by a product that performs consistently at or above the level of customer expectation. The product must support the delivery of the benefit (e.g., Michelin tires must have better safety features for a brand promise based on safety; IBM must have flexible, open, and easy-to-use solutions for its on-demand positioning). Even though emotional aspects of the brand positioning are more fundamental to achieving equity ownership than are rational aspects, the brand cannot win on the emotional plane if the product fails to deliver on functional excellence. Continuous and inspiring innovation is necessary to retain category leadership and expand to higher growth and higher profit categories. Apple's iPod and iTunes are good examples of domain advancement through constant and inspiring innovation.

Communication. Through strategic development and delivery of communications, the brand can develop the equity ownership to achieve LEAP success. Remember, brand equity is a perception in customers' minds. Ownership of brand equity means that customers associate your brand with successfully meeting the high-level need they feel, much more than they associate any competitive brand. Communications and all the touch points of the customers' experience with the brand's products and services build perceptions.

Elio Leoni-Sceti agrees, "Each brand has one primary benefit. As long as the communication builds on the primary benefit it strengthens brand equity. Consistent advertising builds brand equity."

Here are examples of positioning for brand image with one important, high-level emotional benefit:

▶ In water softeners: You can feel smart by protecting your laundry machine so that it will live longer if you use Calgon.

▶ Toilet bowl cleaner: Solves the toilet-cleaning problem, so it reflects positively on the homemaker. "What does the loo say about you?"

The full range of communications is contemplated in this imperative: advertising, public relations, events, in-store promotions, website, Internet viral communications, and personal service.

Channel management. To be successful in delivering end-customer value, the brand must also be successful in delivering value to the channel partner. In packaged goods, that's a retailer like Wal-Mart; in high tech it's a distributor or reseller; in businesses like Mary Kay cosmetics, it's the individuals who represent the brand directly to the consumer; for an online retailer it might be Yahoo! Shopping. By creating value for the channel partner, the brand can obtain superior retail or web presence or "mind share" and improve its opportunity to make sales and realize revenue. By translating the higher-level customer benefit of the brand vision into a higher level of channel partner value, the brand can make the channel a partner in growth. Examples include higher channel margin through premium pricing, the attraction of a higher-spend customer to the retailer's outlets, or the development of storewide programs based on the brand's insights mapped to the channel partner's shopper profile.

A template for a LEAP is illustrated in Figure 6.4 on the following two pages.

TIPS FOR WRITING THE MOST EFFECTIVE LEAP DOCUMENT

1. Do not be afraid to revisit the brand vision and brand challenge. The brand equity framework process is intended to be an iterative process—you may not get the brand vision right the first time, in which case it will require another review of the voice of the customer and customer domain and the options open to the brand in pursuit of equity ownership. Ensure both that the brand ambition is sufficiently stretching, and that it can rationally be achievable over three to five years.

2. The choice of the single equity you seek to own will drive all long-term equity planning and all LEAP imperatives. Is it the highest point on the hierarchy of needs your brand can attain? Can you own it versus competition?

3. You have a choice among all the category-specific equities and general equity drivers where you seek to lead versus competition. Have you chosen the ones that are most important to your customers?

4. The right mix of imperatives should ensure that every brand activity is focused on achieving the financial goals resulting from equity ownership. Typically, imperatives should cover equity ownership via communications, superb customer experience via product development, entering new domains, category growth strategy in current categories, and channel marketing.

5. Are there ways to phase the imperatives so that there is a plan to focus on building a base in the early years of the plan and expanding on that base in the later years? For example, you might concentrate on creating product breakthroughs in the early years, and investing in capturing brand growth with them in the later years.

BRAND LONG-TERM EQUITY APPRECIATION PLAN (LEAP)

Brand/Extension:	Prepared By:	Approved By:
Business Unit:	Date:	Date:
Geography:		

Brand Ambition:	Brand Promise:	Brand Rational/Functional Support:
(Import from Brand Vision Document)	*(Import from Brand Vision Document)*	*(Import from Brand Vision Document)*

Overall LEAP Strategy: Enter a brief summary description of the overall strategy driving the LEAP. The intention is to call out the major direction the brand will take, and the consequent major actions that must be taken to support that direction.

Five-Year Brand Targets

	Year 1	Year 2	Year 3	Year 4	Year 5
Financial Targets:					
Topline Revenues ($M)					
Annual Increase (%)					
Brand Gross Margin ($M)					
Annual Increase (%)					

Commentary:

LEAP Imperatives

LEAP Imperatives are the 5–6 major actions that the brand will undertake to achieve the above targets. They ask, "What do we have to do to meet the Brand Challenge?" Imperatives may differ for each brand, but typically they will fall into these categories: new domain spaces, targeting of consumer changes, product development, product mix changes, communication, and channel management.

Imperative	Measures	Projects
Imperative 1		
Imperative 2		
Imperative 3		
Imperative 4		
Imperative 5		

| | Beginning | | | | | Ending | | | | |
	Group 1	Group 2	Group 3	Group 4	Total	Group 1	Group 2	Group 3	Group 4	Total
BCC Profile Targets:										
% HH										
% Brand Users										
% Brand Revenue										
% Brand Profit										
% Share of Profit Pool										
Brand Units/HH										
Price Paid/Unit ($)										
Gross Margin ($M)										
Marketing Cost ($M)										
Brand Profit/HH										
Total Brand Revenue ($M)										
Total Brand Profit ($M)										
Brand Equity Targets:										
Brand Promise Ownership:										
(Name of Equity)										
Brand Score										
Closest Competitor Score										
Category-Specific Equities:										
Driver 1 (Score)										
Driver 2 (Score)										
Driver 3 (Score)										
General Equity Drivers:										
Different/Unique (Score)										
Relevance (Score)										
Esteem (Score)										
Knowledge (Score)										
Value (Score)										
Loyalty Attitude (Score)										

FIGURE 6.4 LEAP template.

Continuous Refinement of Brand Challenge and LEAP

The initial brand equity development ("Year One" of the five-year LEAP) will properly seek to identify the precise equities for the brand to own, based on a thorough understanding of customers' domains and the customers' hierarchy of needs.

After the identification and articulation of the correct brand equities, execution and measurement against them will follow, guided by the LEAP imperatives. After a defined time period, you will begin to measure the impact of your actions on customers' attitudes and perceptions of your brand. The brand equity monitor (discussed in Chapter 9, "Marketing Metrics: Brand Equity Is Money") will highlight changes in brand equity scores and their correlation with financial performance. The brand commitment profile model will also help you track movements in behavioral loyalty; that is, how shifts in brand equity perceptions are translating into changes in share of requirements.

With these two sets of data in hand, you should revisit your brand challenge and your LEAP. You may assume that your brand vision is correct at this point, and that you have identified the right future path for your brand. If your brand vision needs modification, you should begin the brand equity framework process from step one—with customer insights. However, this is a major re-evaluation and should only be carried out after deep consultation with senior management.

Your brand challenge however, will need to be updated to periodically reflect the gains you have made against the objective—what are the gaps you have narrowed, or even closed this year through execution against the imperatives? Perhaps you have launched a series of new products that enable your brand to better stand for a certain benefit or that meet a certain milestone on the road to your brand ambition. It is unlikely that after one year you have fully met the brand challenge; if you have, then your brand ambition was not stretching enough! But you may have made enough progress to advance the boundaries of the LEAP five-year targets.

Your LEAP will need to be updated with new equity scores and changes in the brand commitment profile. You should be able to assess how well you are doing, and which priorities to rearrange as you go forward into the next time period.

CUSTOMER NEEDS AND PREFERENCES WILL CHANGE OVER TIME

Customers' tastes, habits, and preferences are constantly in flux, and this has been accelerated in recent years by the vast increase in new products in many categories. Consider the proliferation of adult beverages—"premium vodkas," new categories of ready-to-drink, premixed products such as Mike's Hard Lemonade, Smirnoff Ice, and so on. Consumers now find room in their consumption habits for products they would never have considered.

And, to return to the coffee category, look what the growth of Starbucks has done to coffee drinking habits and preferences over the past decade. For the first time in 40 years, young people are becoming coffee drinkers. They are being introduced to new flavors and even new preparation modalities. Every competitor in the coffee category at every level has been required to review its brand vision, its challenge, imperatives, and initiatives. Folgers now offers multiple flavors, even lattes and cappuccinos—items that were probably not on any brand's radar screen 10 years ago.

Therefore, you must constantly monitor customer preferences and behaviors. The boundaries of domains will shift as customers are offered new benefits that enhance their experiences, even within the same categories. Think of the explosion in sports equipment and accessories that have accompanied the rise in mountain bikes, yoga mats, hiking boots, and the like, giving rise to new opportunities for manufacturers to stake out new product and emotional territories.

If you have developed a sound insights process, it will constantly feed into your brand development process, helping you identify, understand, and react to any shifts that occur. Now, that does not mean that you should change your brand vision to match the latest fads. You want to stay on the leading edge of understanding where customers' preferences are heading. This will enable you to evaluate, test, and make bold decisions on new products and benefits that your brand can take advantage of. Moreover, thinking of the customer as a moving target prevents the "lock-in" effect, where benefits and insights are handed down to each new member of the brand team, seemingly unchallengeable.

Each year you will need to assess your progress against the brand vision, and update your brand challenge document and LEAP accordingly. These should then be shared and inculcated as part of the annual planning process.

SUMMARY

The LEAP provides the vehicle for linking brand imperatives and initiatives into an actionable blueprint for building brand equity based on the brand vision and brand challenge. All aspects of brand-building imperatives including advancing into new domain spaces, new product, service and solution development, brand commitment profile enhancement, and communication and channel management, should be considered. While there are many valid models for choosing metrics, the marketing managers should have the responsibility to help fashion the metrics that are right for the brand and have them adopted by senior management.

PROCESSES FOR BRAND IMPLEMENTATION

Greatness lies in implementation. This section details how the enterprise marketing management revolution can help you ensure functional and executional excellence.

Chapter 7

Building a Plan with an Integrated Marketing Strategy

Chapter 8

Functional Excellence

BUILDING A PLAN WITH AN INTEGRATED MARKETING STRATEGY

➤ *Why do you need an integrated marketing strategy?*

➤ *How do you create an integrated marketing strategy?*

➤ *How can you measure spending effectiveness?*

➤ *How can you improve spending efficiency?*

➤ *How can you best allocate spending for maximum return?*

One of the great challenges in marketing management is assembling the right combination of vehicles to deliver the objective at the lowest possible cost. The optimal solution almost always requires a range of complementary elements and the question becomes: "What's the right balance of ingredients?" Under some conditions, marketers have powerful new weapons, such as market mix modeling and agent-based modeling to help answer the question of spending allocation. But under all conditions, marketers can enhance their chances of obtaining the right answer by adopting what we call "integrated marketing strategy" . . . what others call "cascading choices."

The principles are simple: (1) understand the objectives of each initiative clearly, (2) build a "custom" solution by choosing marketing vehicles in descending order of their capability in achieving the goal, and (3) never underspend on a higher-priority vehicle in order to find funding for a lower-priority vehicle.

WHY DO YOU NEED AN INTEGRATED MARKETING STRATEGY?

Traditional marketing models are dissolving rapidly because there are so many more touch points for marketers to consider. The range is baffling. Brands today are built via the Internet touch point, the doctor's office visit, the phone call to the 800 number, sports sponsorship, and advertising delivered via the car radio while the customer drives to work in the morning, to name but a few. The traditional marketing weaponry—the mass market TV campaign in B2C and the direct sales force in B2B—are delivering lower returns on the high investment cost required to sustain them.

If you are managing a B2C brand, the mass market TV vehicle no longer communicates your message to your target consumers with the same efficiency. The way customers capture and process information relevant to marketing has changed more in the past decade than at any other period since the post-WWII development of TV as the primary advertising medium. If you are managing a B2B brand, the returns from person-to-person selling can't keep pace with the cost of keeping a sales force on message with all the latest data required to support solution marketing via relationship management.

Mass marketing has also become relatively expensive. Over the last 20 years, while annual inflation is up less than 5 percent, the annual increase in the cost of television advertising is closer to 10 percent. All these factors are changing the dynamics of how organizations view targeted marketing, which provides better value and the ability to more accurately measure the return on investment for each element in the marketing mix.

Market mix modeling breaks the trap of the one media vehicle or targeting approach strategy that inhibits marketing resource allocation effectiveness. At one end of the strategy spectrum are mass marketing and the direct sales force, both artifacts of the 1950s. At the other end of the spectrum is "one-to-one" marketing, which has also proven to be flawed. Direct mail response rates for consumer financial services are at an all-time low because of the category's abuse of the medium, and only a handful of major brands (like Dell and Amazon) have demonstrated the appropriate understanding of the brand imperative to develop the customized selling capability via the Internet to the point of achieving critical mass.

But in between these extremes there are a host of opportunities to increase the efficiency and effectiveness of brand building by eschewing the wasteful "empty calories" of mass marketing and substituting the "protein-and-fitness" regimen of sophisticated, scientific targeting. Targeting is an element of marketing strategy that, too often, is paid mere lip service. A little thoughtfulness and analysis would go a long way to making your media, direct-to-customer, promotion, and PR dollars significantly more effective and efficient. CEOs should harness every stimulus for improved targeting to accelerate brand growth.

THE ADVANTAGES OF AN INTEGRATED MARKETING STRATEGY

An integrated marketing strategy (IMS) will address the issues created by a blinkered approach to marketing. The IMS will integrate the efforts of the relevant marketing functions to deliver the results for the brand. The IMS will:

▶ Start with a clear identification of the initiative that the brand is trying to achieve and the objectives related to that initiative.

▶ Identify the extent to which each marketing function will help achieve an initiative's objective and the role that each function will play.

▶ Use existing customer knowledge and insights to create a strategy that addresses the marketing task at hand.

▶ Develop the strategy without getting into the tactics of how each function will deliver its share of the objective.

▶ Identify the optimum marketing spending to help achieve the objectives.

The following is a real-world example of an IMS:

Folgers coffee has a clear strategic imperative that can be stated, "to dominate the morning coffee drinking occasion." This strategic imperative would reflect intensive analysis of coffee drinking patterns, revealing a dramatic long-term erosion in coffee drinking over the past 40 years. That erosion, however, has been much more severe in coffee drinking occasions other than breakfast. The morning "shot" of caffeine continues to have broad-based consumer appeal. Once Folgers brand management determined that the morning coffee drinking occasion offers the largest "profit pool" compared with other coffee drinking occasions, the company would begin a methodical analysis of the morning coffee occasion data such as size, growth, number of cups of coffee consumed per morning, type of coffee, consumption location, and the like. They would also analyze the morning coffee drinkers themselves: demographics, annual economic worth as a coffee consumer, attitudes toward coffee drinking, purchase habits, and so on.

From this analysis should emerge a series of actions, or initiatives, that are required to turn the strategic intent of Folgers brand dominance of market share of morning coffee drinking into marketplace reality.

Notice that the imperative is defined through purposeful analysis of data that is driven by the insight that the morning breakfast occasion is the time when the greatest number of coffee drinkers value their cup of coffee the most. By understanding this insight and what coffee in the morning "means" to coffee drinkers, Folgers can create its brand initiatives or marketing actions to capitalize on this insightful truth about the coffee category and its users.

P&G would start by examining every weapon in its marketing armory to ascertain the appropriate choices. For example, they would start with positioning and the translation of the brand promise into an actual campaign execution ("the best part of waking up is Folgers in your cup"), widely believed by P&G insiders to be one of the best pieces of advertising copy developed by the company in the last 50 years.

They would look at media to ascertain what kind of media vehicles, media weight, and media schedule would have the most impact on the consumer's decision regarding the morning coffee drinking occasion.

They would examine customers' brand loyalty (percent of coffee annual requirements satisfied by Folgers) to ascertain what kind of promotional pattern would generate the most leverage given the consumer's purchase patterns. Lastly, they would look at the retail trade to understand the role of coffee in the retail trade's merchandising plans and how they could align their brand's strategic intent with the retailer's plan and the consumer's purchasing patterns for coffee.

This aspect of the Folgers IMS deserves closer scrutiny. P&G has established a long-range target for volume and share for Folgers coffee. That long-range target is built around an easily understandable model that has two metrics: household penetration or trial, and share of requirements, also called loyalty. Figure 7.1 shows a brand that has 50 percent penetration and 40 percent share of total requirements; that is, among the 50 percent of the households who tried the brand at least once in the past year, the brand accounted for a 40 percent share of the coffee drunk within those households. (The mathematically astute will note that this amounts to a 20 percent share of the total coffee market).

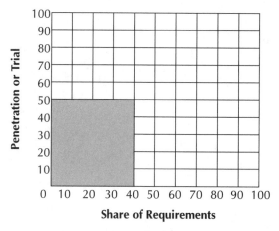

FIGURE 7.1 Penetration vs. share of requirements.

A marketer has two fairly clear choices for increasing volume. One is to increase market penetration (the percentage of coffee-using households that try the brand in a year); the other is to increase brand loyalty or share of requirements within the households that try the brand.

Folgers has been tried over the past 30 years by virtually every coffee drinker. Also, given that brand loyalty among the majority of coffee drinkers is relatively low, the best choice for increasing volume appears to be by increasing share of requirements from 40 percent to 50 percent or, in other words, to increase Folgers consumption within current Folger buying households by 25 percent.

Therefore, the marketing objective facing Folgers is to increase share of requirements. But what marketing vehicle is best configured to address this share of requirements objective? One answer might be in the size of the package the consumer purchases. The typical consumer is a female homemaker who purchases about 18 pounds of coffee annually. If that consumer purchases coffee in one-pound lots, she will make 18 purchase decisions in a year. The retail supermarket coffee category in one-pound tins or packages has a relatively low customer loyalty, and is highly price promoted because most brands are perceived to be commodities. From data available to the brand, Folgers can calculate that it has about one chance in three to win the next one-pound purchase of a consumer who bought Folgers the last time she purchased coffee.

However, if the marketer is able to shift the consumer purchase preference from a one-pound bag to a three-pound can or from two pounds to six pounds, the number of purchase occasions where the consumer can switch to another brand is reduced. Also, market research has confirmed that the loyalty in a home trading up in its average purchase size shifts dramatically in favor of the brand driving the trade up. For example, if the average household has a 33 percent loyalty to Folgers at the beginning of any given year and Folgers is able to get that household to purchase six pounds of coffee at the beginning of the year, they have already equaled their annual average loyalty with this one purchase (6 pounds divided by 18 = 33 percent). Just one more purchase of any size (one, two, three, four, or six pounds) will increase Folgers's share of requirements in that household for the entire year.

Folgers has successfully implemented this tactic over the past several years. They have increased promotion focus on larger sizes, often by encouraging large chain stores that account for high retail market penetration (such as Wal-Mart) to offer large-size promotions. This has, in turn, shifted the promotion pressure from smaller sizes to larger sizes and improved Folgers position as the preferred large-size package in many households. This tactic, in concert with effective copy and a creative media plan, exemplifies the kind of focused, choiceful integrated marketing strategy we espouse.

THE INTEGRATED MARKETING STRATEGY PROCESS

A great IMS has the following:

- A well-defined target customer
- Detailed customer knowledge and learning
- Clearly defined initiatives with measurable objectives
- A clear description of the marketing task at hand
- Synergistic functional strategies

> ▶ The ability to make cascading choices and not try to do too much with too few resources

> ▶ The ability to be flexible and adopt to market changes

Table 7.1 outlines the process for developing an integrated marketing strategy for a brand.

TABLE 7.1 Integrated Marketing Strategy Process

#	Process Step	Comments
1	Identify and profile the potential target customer segment(s) for each of the initiatives.	The "who" of each initiative is not just a demographic segment but also contains information on their attitudes, behavioral traits, and any relevant customer knowledge and insights.
2	Prioritize the segments for actioning the initiatives (if relevant).	The potential segments are prioritized based on size, competitive strength, appeal of initiative offering, past history of the brand with the customer segment, and strategic interest of the segment to the brand.
3	Identify the attitudinal barriers to make the behavior change in customers.	Identifying the attitudinal barriers focuses the team on the task at hand and assists in short-listing the marketing vehicles.
4	Shortlist marketing vehicles accordingly.	The marketing vehicles are shortlisted based on the task at hand, available budget, and initiative timing.
5	Review integrated strategy options.	These are the "cascading choices"—among marketing vehicles based on the understanding of the objective and the effectiveness and efficiency of each marketing vehicle in meeting similar objectives in the past. Choices are filtered through budget constraints. The conceptually "best" choice will not work if there is not enough budget to reach critical mass. In that case, choose the next best option that can be fully funded. Also consider results that indicate that two options working together are more effective than either one on its own—the 1+1=3 phenomenon. For example, a sales call plus a free sample might deliver more penetration gains than either option on its own.
6	Select the appropriate IMS.	If two or more vehicles are very similar in their ability to support the intiative, or if there are potential synergies in using more than one vehicle, allocate marketing dollars to marketing vehicles using market mix modeling or agent-based modeling.

MARKET MIX MODELING: HOW TO BE EFFECTIVE AND EFFICIENT IN ALLOCATING MARKETING RESOURCES

A critical issue facing brand managers is the optimal allocation of funds among a wide range of spending options. We have reviewed best practices across dozens of companies. No company seems to have a comprehensive, holistic, integrated approach to address this basic requirement of marketing management. Most companies impose some primitive fiscal discipline. They do not explore each component of the plan and apply a rigorous reasoning to each one, model the trade-offs, and then allocate funds across the alternatives to maximize profitability.

There are several reasons for this failure. The most common is the excuse, "We don't have the data." This begs the question, "Why not?" Isn't it the responsibility of marketing to develop the data that enables responsible fund allocation? One of the significant failures of modern marketing leadership is its unwillingness to spend $250,000 to get adequate market mix modeling data and its simultaneous willingness to spend $20,000,000 on marketing without adequate models or data.

Scholarly dissertations have been written on the strengths and weaknesses of market mix modeling. Suffice it to say that the cost, complexity, and admitted limitations of the technique have often discouraged marketers from making the financial and intellectual effort to use this powerful tool.

This lack of determination by marketing management to utilize this tool is remarkable given the fact that the cost of a market mix modeling study is generally 1 percent or less of what a typical company spends to support a major brand. The simplest math would indicate that a market mix model study would pay out with less than a 1 percent improvement in the spending allocation of a brand. Yet many CEOs, CFOs, and marketing managers are simply unwilling to make that expenditure. Their resistance should be decreasing every day, especially in business verticals such as financial services, pharmaceuticals, telecommunications, and retail, where rich and highly granular data facilitates the most sophisticated analysis.

NO HALF WASTED

One criticism of market mix modeling is that it is dependent on masses of time series data that are not available for many of the more unusual and contemporary marketing vehicles.

That being said, adopting an integrated marketing approach has recently been made easier by the application of a new modeling technique—agent-based modeling. Chances are that your children are familiar with agent-based modeling in the form of popular simulation games such as Sim City. These games employ principles of agent-based modeling that are also used by the Department of Defense to do "war gaming" and by others in various academic pursuits such as sociology and cultural anthropology.

Agent-based modeling may someday be the subject of another book. At this point in time, we would point out that leading-edge marketers such as P&G and Pepsi are beginning to utilize agent-based modeling precisely because it enables them to model virtually all marketing inputs—without the data limitations imposed by traditional market mix modeling—and to rank order the relative contribution of these inputs to share and profit gains. Figure 7.2, provided by Decision Power, one of the leading exponents of agent-based modeling, shows the relative value of various forms of market mix modeling for any brand or business.

	Statistical Regression	Conjoint	Test Marketing	MarketSim (Agent-Based)
Explains market dynamics (customer, channel, and competitor behavior)	Few	Some	Some	Many
Adaptability to change (power to forecast market when the future is not like the past)	Low	Medium	Medium	High
Scope (dimensions of "What-If?" analysis)	Low (mass media & price)	Low (attributes)	Medium (all variables)	High (all variables)
Questions addressed per model (profit, share, ROI, sales, media planning, brand portfolio optimization, competitive strategy, etc.)	Few	Few	Several	All
Breadth of market behaviors modeled (awareness, trial, share, media flighting response, mix synergy, etc.)	None	Few	Most	Most
Accuracy within scope	High	High	High	High
Use of data (Time Series, consumer survey, assumptions, rules of thumb, etc.)	Some	Some	All	All
Cost per project/question (software plus consulting)	Medium	Medium	High	Low

FIGURE 7.2 Agent-based modeling vs. alternative techniques.

SUMMARY

Each marketing initiative requires a customized solution that we call an integrated marketing strategy. That strategy is characterized by a clear target consumer, rigorous goals, and a considered weighing of the ability of a specific tactic to meet the goals. Under optimal circumstances, advanced techniques such as market mix modeling or the newer agent-based modeling can help marketers arrive at the proper balance among numerous marketing alternatives. In the absence of such tools, an orderly process such as the one advocated here ("cascading choices") will yield an improved result for virtually all marketers. This is the technique being used to great effect by the world's most sophisticated marketers in venues where data is scarce and advanced tools impractical.

chapter 8

FUNCTIONAL EXCELLENCE

> ➤ *How can marketing management ensure that the best strategies are executed excellently?*
>
> ➤ *How can one marketing leader develop excellence across a diverse panorama of functions?*

Excellence in marketing requires familiarity with a broad panorama of academic disciplines, from psychology to anthropology, from sociology to economics and finance. Indeed, many marketers were originally attracted to marketing as a profession precisely because it covers such a broad swathe of the human experience. It's certainly not narrow and rarely boring!

Just as marketing covers a broad range of academic disciplines, its successful execution requires a similarly broad range of functional skills. And herein lies another challenge. The best strategies can be negated by poor execution caused by functional failures. Yet few marketing leaders possess the capacity and stamina to master the intricacies of all the diverse functions of modern marketing, including:

- New product and service development
- Package or store design
- Retail loyalty card marketing
- Advertising creative development/agency relations
- Advertising production
- Media buying including emerging new media
- Merchandising at the point of sale

- Direct marketing including e-marketing
- Building brand equity through the sales force
- Customer promotion
- Event marketing and endorsements
- PR
- Market research and market mix modeling
- Training

Each of these takes years to master and when one feels that the subject has been mastered, change often intervenes to introduce uncertainty. (Ask marketers how the growth of the Internet has affected their customer relationships.) So, each functional expert has his own experience of "Zeno's Paradox" as the goal of perfect knowledge always recedes from view with each individual step forward in functional skill.

If the functional experts themselves must keep learning in a dynamic, continuously expanding universe, how can an individual marketing leader possibly master such a diverse functional environment?

The answer is "You can't." That's one reason we wrote this book—to help you manage a complex and diverse set of functional skills that defy the personal mastery of the ordinary mortal. Your job is to make all of your functional experts better because no matter how good you are as an individual marketer, you will almost always lose in the marketplace to the marketing leader who has raised the capabilities of his or her functional experts across the entire department.

This brings us back to the issue: how can one marketing leader create functional excellence across the increasingly complex multi-disciplinary array of functional skills required by marketing in the 21st century?

As is so often the case, the answer to that challenge is to ask the right questions. We recommend that marketing leaders ask each of their functional experts the following questions:

Do you have a process?

- If so, can you show it to me step by step? Who owns the process and the steps therein?
- What are the key inputs in your process?
- Are you getting the high-quality input you need to produce superior outputs?

▶ Where is the process working well/poorly? Why?

▶ Do those responsible for inputs understand their responsibilities?

▶ Does everyone on your functional team know the process?

▶ Do our third-party external suppliers understand our process and align with it?

▶ When is the last time you changed the process?

Do you know and communicate "best practice" throughout your department?

▶ Identify the three most important tasks regularly performed by your function.

▶ Do you have a best practice example for these tasks?

▶ Do you train your people systematically in the best practice process and the latest learning?

▶ Do our third-party suppliers have best practice examples?

▶ Show me examples of how our output reflects "best practice."

▶ What do our competitors do differently in your function?

▶ When is the last time we changed a "best practice?" What drove that change?

How do you measure performance in your functional area?

▶ Upon what metrics should the company evaluate your function's performance?

▶ Are these measures of inputs or measures of output (effectiveness) of your function?

▶ How are these metrics trending?

What are we doing to improve your function's contribution?

▶ What tests are we running?

▶ What are the most important external changes affecting your function?

- What is the most important thing you wish you knew about your functional environment?
- How are we using new technology?
- What's the most important change we have made in your function in the last three years?

The answers to these questions will help your functional leadership know what you expect from them and provide you with a diagnostic about what you can expect from them. Now here are several specific steps you can take to ensure functional excellence.

1. Provide your functions with a Marketing Knowledge Center.

Every function will perform better if its members have a panoramic understanding of the business plus access to best practice examples across the spectrum of marketing, and not just in their own functional area. The function may have its own "pages" within the company's marketing knowledge center, but should also focus on understanding the entire brand-building process and not just their part in it. In addition, web links to functionally specific thought leading sites are a good way to keep functional leaders thinking about improvement. For example, numerous links are readily available to websites on consumer research and modeling where any one could receive all the necessary background on new developments such as agent-based modeling. Many trade and academic organizations run excellent websites on subjects such as forecasting. Yahoo has industry- and discipline-specific chat rooms that are valuable information sources and stimuli.

2. Use functional "landscape reports" to stimulate functional improvement.

These reports have many benefits in the overall EMM Way of Brand Building. Their primary benefit is to align all functional groups around a common view of reality so that planning can proceed on a sound factual basis. But one of the greatest values of the landscape is causing functional leadership to take a look in the mirror and report what's new in their function and to identify what they don't know (the "I wish I knews").

3. Communicate the long-term equity appreciation plan (LEAP) and the brand challenge.

Constantly require that every function's plans and practices reinforce the brand's equity. The most functionally expert department in your company is virtually useless if it isn't pulling its oar in the agreed strategic direction. One way to encourage functional alignment is to create a master creative brief and share it with every function. In a large, marketing-intensive organization that creates millions of customer contacts every day with everything from TV commercials to sales presentations and product data sheets, it is imperative that every customer touch be driven by a common master creative brief stipulating core message elements, tonality, logo presentation, and so on. That is the only way to multiply the message by thousands of employees.

Shown below is a comprehensive guide to the concept of the "Master Creative Brief." This document exemplifies how EMM Group teaches key concepts to its clients. These documents are converted to HTML and become a permanent training document available 24/7 within the company's Marketing Knowledge Center.

MASTER CREATIVE BRIEF: CONCEPTUAL GUIDANCE

The Master Creative Brief is one example of a process tool that ensures functional excellence in implementation by standardizing the inputs for creative marketing projects. It translates your Brand Vision into a concise and specific development framework to guide Functional Teams in developing their contribution to IMS.

One of its primary roles is to ensure that the immense brand-building power of consumer insights (as captured in the Voice of the Customer) is carried through in a consistent manner into creative communications of all kinds.

It includes a frame of reference, customer insights summary statement, brand promise, support and brand character, and is deliberately written in simple, bare-bones language.

Finalizing the Master Creative Brief is the input to the start of functional development plans.

Sections

Introduction to Master Creative Brief

Components of the Master Creative Brief

Functions of the Master Creative Brief

Sections in Detail

Introduction to Master Creative Brief

The Master Creative Brief translates your Brand Vision into a concise and specific development framework that will be used by all internal functional groups who implement the brand's communications strategy. Serving as the transition from the Voice of the Customer, Customer Domain research, and Brand Equity planning stages to the annual plan development and planning stage, the Master Creative Brief directs strategic creative development and ultimately dictates the success of your resulting communications and initiatives.

Deliberately precise, the Master Creative Brief is written in simple, bare-bones language. This ensures that each word is carefully considered, and communicates a meaningful, useful direction to the agencies and other users.

The following diagram illustrates how the Master Creative Brief fits into your overall marketing strategy. Note that the Brand Vision drives the Master Creative Brief that, in turn, becomes the foundation for your Customer Communications Strategy Briefs developed at the initiative level by the functional teams. Successfully executing these initial processes will help you achieve winning results in your functional strategies and projects.

The Master Creative Brief is the most important input you have in guiding functional groups' creative direction across all external brand communications.

Senior representatives of the brand and the functional teams will approve and sign off on the Master Creative Brief before any creative development can begin.

Components of the Master Creative Brief

The Master Creative Brief draws from the Voice of the Customer and Brand Vision documents for the key components:

> ▶ Frame of Reference: The Brand Ambition sets the context for the overall communications task at hand. It describes where you want to take the brand. You should also describe the expectations that you have of communications in helping you achieve the Brand Ambition.

▶ Customer Insights: A very brief summary of the key customer insight that drives the Brand Ambition and must infuse all communications.

▶ Target Audience: Taken from the Brand Vision document, the Target Audience describes in words who your brand advertising will appeal to.

▶ Brand Promise: The high-level emotional benefit and/or brand equity that you are seeking to own. Taken from the Brand Vision document.

▶ Rationale/Support: The emotional and functional reasons-to-believe your brand can offer the Brand Promise. Taken from the Brand Vision document.

▶ Brand Character: How your brand will express itself, its tone and character. Again, taken from the Brand Vision document.

▶ Executional Elements: Key brand elements that should be included in all communications. Usually confined to logos, iconic elements, and sometimes taglines. Importantly, the executional elements should be reconsidered over time as you learn more about your brand and its appeal to your customers, but should not be changed with each execution.

Functions of the Master Creative Brief

The Master Creative Brief meets these key functions:

▶ Joint agreement: The Master Creative Brief spells out the brand's direction and focus. In tune with the Brand Vision, the MCB clarifies and aligns viewpoints between you, your functional departments and agencies, and multiple layers of management, enabling you to better positively influence the creative development direction.

▶ Source document: Clear and concise, this provides the necessary background without too much detail, so that the functional teams can start generating ideas. Most important, it illustrates how the brand's overarching vision translates into specific objectives for an individual project.

▶ Insights transfer: The MCB ensures that there is a continuous thread linking Customer Insights (the brand's most powerful source of added value and competitive advantage) and customer communications.

▶ Evaluation tool: The Master Creative Brief continues to be a significant tool even beyond the initiation of creative development. Since the first presentation of creative ideas can take place several weeks later, the Master Creative Brief acts as a quick refresher before reviewing and commenting on creative work.

▶ Intellectual property: Over time, the Master Creative Brief is often one of the few sources of historical perspective behind individual advertising and communications executions. This can be a helpful source of past advertising strategies, key insights, and approaches to common situations (launches, competitive threats, etc.). Actual business results can be correlated to factors captured in the creative strategy. From these, you can draw conclusions about what should be reapplied in the future.

Understanding the power of your creative strategy can help you lock onto successful results in your marketing projects.

4. Require your functional leadership to capture "best practice" and make it available on the Marketing Knowledge Center.

In business, speed of learning is the only truly sustainable competitive advantage, yet most companies have no process and no mechanism for identifying, capturing, and then redeploying "best practice." The key to functional excellence is knowing what has worked. Unfortunately, most companies do not systematically capture and build on this learning. They begin every year by turning to a new, blank page, ignoring past mistakes and successes. If they have learned, it's often through trial and error captured by the fragile and undependable memories of individual employees who regularly leave their immediate job, leave the company altogether, or simply retire with a lifetime of wisdom.

The resistance among functional leaders to capture best practice, to codify it, and then to share it through technology and training is one of the great mysteries of business. At some perverse and possibly unconscious level, the resistance reflects the leadership's desire to magnify their own personal importance by arrogating all authority under the penumbra of their own ego. If no best practice has been identified and stored, the only best practice is what the leader says it is. For whatever reason, that is the prevailing condition in many companies. You can test our assertion: go to your functional leaders and ask them to show you best practice in their most important activities.

This problem has grown exponentially as business has become a culture of face-to-face meetings entertained by presentations with funny face symbols and indecipherable graphs rather than one driven by tightly reasoned written memos with tables of supporting data and page upon page of written documentation attached.

In the functionally excellent marketing department, best practice is available 24/7 on a marketing knowledge center. A lesson learned and proven by experience is captured, vetted, approved, and mounted on the MKC.

5. Ensure that the functions know the target customer and how they touch him.

Every function touches the target in various ways. Every touch is an opportunity to reinforce brand equity and to SELL. That's why Wal-Mart has turned its trucks into billboards. The major hotel chains are getting good at optimizing touches. Their management realizes that the employees with the most frequent customer contact are the desk clerks, maids, and waiters—among the lowest paid employees in the enterprise. That's why today, it is virtually impossible to exit your hotel room in a well-run chain without receiving a cheery greeting from not only the front-line employees, but also the maids waiting in the hall to tidy the rooms.

The savviest of marketers, P&G, recently executed a collective corporate forehead slap when they realized that they were not optimizing one of their most important touches, the contact between the consumer and the package at the store shelf. Other marketers agree. That's why packaging and visual merchandising, previously somewhat of a wasteland, have become among the most dynamic and exciting functions in package goods marketing.

6. Expect every function to provide an ROI on its expenditures.

P&G has publicly announced its intention to develop an ROI measure on every marketing-related expenditure from in-store merchandising to sponsorships to PR. This may at first glance seem impractical or even impossible but it underscores the seriousness of this large, sophisticated, and determined marketer. Sadly, it also indicates how derelict marketing has been in demanding ROI measures from itself when virtually every other major corporate function has been required to meet some returns measure for decades. Traditionally, marketing functions, especially those without readily available third-party data, have claimed ignorance or impossibility when asked to provide an ROI or metric of any kind. Now marketers are becoming quite creative in providing metrics when a determined manager simply refuses to fund someone's favorite but immeasureable idea. Don't you imagine that Wal-Mart was able to measure the impressions and even model awareness shifts associated with their moving truck billboards?

7. Create a process to stimulate and reward functional improvement.

Ask each functional leader on an annual basis to present two things to their functional leadership peers: (a) the most important new development in their discipline over the past 12 months, and (b) the most important change that his function has made for your company. Have the functional peers choose the function that has made the most important change. Recognize that change financially and publicize it internally.

8. Reach out for external stimulus.

Demand that your functional leaders go to conferences and submit written reports on their learnings. Ask them to arrange for presentations by suppliers, consultants, and customers regarding functional issues of mutual importance.

9. Make each function better by enforcing collaboration through process.

Functional excellence is the second most desirable goal of any marketing organization. The most desirable is total marketing excellence characterized by building brand equity, delivering the annual profit goal, and adding to the understanding of the target consumer. The goal of individual functional excellence makes sense only in the context of the larger goal of overall excellence. Therefore, marketing leadership must ensure the functional collaboration to produce the higher goal. The key to collaboration is a process that embodies it. The integrated marketing process is the business tool to achieve this goal, and common metrics represent the supporting discipline that creates an atmosphere of collaboration by leveling the playing field.

SUMMARY

Functional excellence can be institutionalized through a rigorous process of self examination, benchmarking, analysis and archiving best practices. Marketing leadership can create functional excellence across the diverse skill base of modern marketing by a process of questioning augmented by the practices and tools discussed above. The essence of marketing leadership is making everyone in the department better by demanding the functional excellence that builds brand equity, the primary responsibility of the marketer.

part IV

THE SUPPORTING INFRASTRUCTURE: METRICS, TECHNOLOGY AND TRAINING

Marketing lacks the robust infrastructure developed for the supply chain over the last twenty years. In this part, we show how to build the infrastructure with the right technology, how to tune it with the right metrics, and how to train and motivate the marketing community.

chapter 9

MARKETING METRICS: BRAND EQUITY IS MONEY

> ➤ *What are the most important metrics to guide your plan to achieve your objectives?*
>
> ➤ *How do you know you are making good progress toward achieving your objectives?*
>
> ➤ *What is the best marketing model for your business?*

The element of marketing that generates the most confused thinking is metrics. We intend to clarify that confusion by suggesting some simple rules.

1. Metrics should focus on outcomes and how they are achieved.
2. Metrics should be composed within a shared framework.
3. The approach should be from the top down and not the bottom up.
4. Effectiveness should take precedence over efficiency.

MARKETING OUTCOMES: BRAND EQUITY IS MONEY

The purpose of marketing is to create or change attitudes that lead to desirable behavior. The outcome of doing so is that more customers buy more of your brand of goods or services at more favorable prices. There are a number of ways of looking at this outcome from the CEO's viewpoint:

▶ **Value creation.** The net present value of the future cash flows from brand building translates into brand value that, in turn, translates into increased shareholder value, which is the CEO's main job. We saw in Chapter 1 that brand strength and brand stature result in EVA growth.

▶ **Cash flow.** Strong brands improve cash flows in four ways—higher, faster, longer, less risky. Free cash flow or EBITDA (earnings before interest, tax, depreciation, and amortization) growth would be another way of measuring brand-building outcomes.

▶ **Gross margins.** One way of looking at brand-building outcomes is the higher gross margin that brands can achieve by commanding a premium price over alternative customer choices and by achieving a mix of customer purchases (for example, a product line that is 75 percent "regular price" and 25 percent "premium price") that delivers, on balance, a higher margin. We saw in Chapter 6 how Reckitt Benckiser achieves this outcome with their "Virtuous Cycle" approach.

There are examples of all of these outcomes metrics in use, but in the end we opt for the simplest of choices: top-line revenue growth and gross margin.

Top-line revenue growth is the purest measure of marketing outcomes because that is marketing's job. Selling more goods and services to more customers at more favorable prices drives top-line revenue growth. Put more elegantly, we say that brand building makes your brand more relevant to more people in more parts of their (personal or business) lives, but it amounts to the same thing in terms of outcomes.

The top-line revenue growth metric can be refined in several ways. One is to look at *net* revenue growth. The word "net" implies that we have taken away some cost burden. In the case of marketing, many companies take away the costs of discounts to the customer to make the final sale. In a sense, marketing is responsible for the discounts, because the stronger the brand, the fewer and lower the discounts. Now, this isn't always true. Sales and accounting come up with many arcane ways to massage the difference between the list price and the net price. However, marketers should not resist the measurement of net revenues as their outcome, as opposed to gross revenues.

A second way is to look at revenue growth versus a baseline. This is truly marketing's focus. In year one of a brand's life, all revenue is growth revenue, and, in that year, marketing can rightly take credit for having directed the development of a brand that customers needed, and made them aware of it and induced trial and initial repeat purchase. In subsequent years, it is the growth in revenue for which marketing should take responsibility. The best way to look at this is growth versus baseline, or *carryover*. This measure assumes that there would be some level of revenue even if marketing did nothing to support the brand in the current year. Anything above that baseline level is the net positive effect of the incremental marketing support in that year. (This approach also accommodates those painful situations where a brand is in secular decline. If you ask your marketers to continue to offer the brand to customers, they should be measured on revenues over baseline; if the baseline is declining and the marketers are successful in slowing down the decline, then they should be recognized for it.)

In addition to net revenue growth or growth over baseline revenue, a third outcome measure for marketing should be the increase in gross margin achieved by improved pricing and mix. This should be expressed in revenue terms rather than percentage terms. This is depicted in Figure 9.1.

The brand equity monitor business model.

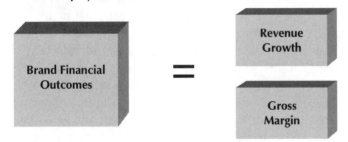

FIGURE 9.1 Define desired financial outcomes.

So, at the end of the year, marketing is measured by the increase in net top-line revenue and gross margin dollars. That's another way of saying: *brand equity is money*. Notice that we haven't focused on market share as an outcome, for many reasons. First, you can't take market share to the bank, so it's not truly an outcome. Second, the achievement of share is not truly in the marketer's hands; there are a lot of exogenous variables that are beyond the control of the marketing department. Third, share is often achieved by sacrificing unit price and gross margin (i.e., "buying share of market" via deep discounting); this is fatal to brand building and the opposite of what marketing should be trying to achieve. Fourth, share is an outmoded concept in the era of domain strategy. When P&G's Crest brand is in the business of toothpaste, toothbrushes, whitening strips, breath mints, and floss, what is the market for which you compute share? Oral-centered self-confidence is a domain, but you'd be hard-pressed to compute a share of domain. The same is true for Dell brand in the desktop, laptop, networking, services, digital imaging, camera, and TV markets.

THE METRICS FRAMEWORK

By a framework, we mean a structured concept of how the brand-building process works. This provides both a common understanding throughout the company, and a shared acceptance of what are the right metrics for the framework.

The right framework follows the structure in Figure 9.2.

Financial outcomes are driven by the strength of brand equity. Brand equity is driven by three major influences: innovation, communication, and brand touch. Each of these drivers should have its own metrics. An ideal brand equity building model should be able to allocate spending between these three major groups of activities in proportion to their measured contribution to building brand equity. Agent-based modeling (see Chapter 7) is capable of delivering this level of understanding.

You will also need an intermediate model between the brand equity score and the measure of financial outcomes that you select. When you walk into the CFO's office and declare that the brand equity score you have devised is a direct driver of top-line revenue growth and gross margin, your CFO is going to pause; his/her training doesn't allow him/her to understand the direct nature of that relationship. He/She needs the help of an intermediate construct, which we call the *brand commitment profile*. It's the metric that captures the idea of more customers buying more of your brand's offerings at more favorable prices.

The brand commitment profile is the metric for the most simple yet profound question in marketing: are my financial outcomes better if I maintain loyalty with my current customers or if I spend my funds on attracting new customers? A preponderance of analytical evidence points to the fact that loyal customers are the most profitable. (To cite just one example, a well-known 1990 *Harvard Business Review* article by Frederick Reichheld and Earl Sasser indicated that "companies can boost profits by almost 100% by retaining just 5% more of their customers.")

The brand equity monitor business model.

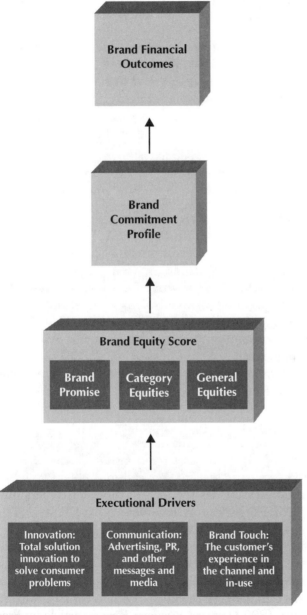

FIGURE 9.2 The brand equity monitor framework.

But there are times in a brand's life when it must emphasize the acquisition of those customers rather than their retention. The brand commitment profile is built on the proposition that:

1. Attitude drives (precedes) behavior. Therefore we must first build positive attitudes to the brand. We call this *affective commitment*—customers love and trust the brand so much that they will buy it at every opportunity, pay more for it (e.g., by not seeking out the deepest of discounts or the lowest cost channel), and give favorable consideration to every new product the brand offers.

2. The resultant behavior is loyalty, defined as *share of requirements*—of all the dollars the customer spends in the target category, the loyal customer allocates all or most of them to your brand.

The brand commitment profile is depicted in Figure 9.3.

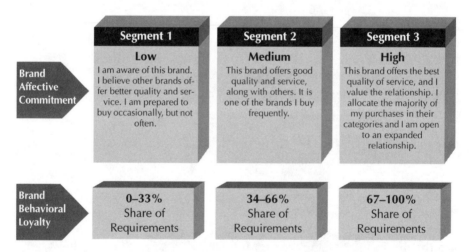

FIGURE 9.3 The brand commitment profile.

So now our metrics framework is complete:

1. Measure outcomes: top-line revenue growth and gross margin.

2. The driver of these outcomes is the brand commitment profile; how many customers are in the low-, medium-, and high-affective commitment segments and what percentage share of their requirements your brand achieves.

3. The driver of affective commitment is brand equity, expressed as a brand equity score.

4. The drivers of the brand equity score are the marketing programs in the three major "boxes" of innovation, communications, and brand touch.

THE MEASURES

Top-line revenue growth and gross margin. These measures come directly from your internal reporting systems. Data integration can bring them directly to the marketer's desktop in a dashboard that monitors brand performance.

Affective commitment or brand attitude. This measure comes from survey data. It is a lot different from customer satisfaction, which is merely a snapshot in time of how the customer feels today. It captures the idea of both historical experience and future commitment. The question can be captured as brand trust or as a five-point scale question from "I would never consider this brand" to "I am totally committed to this brand and expect both to stay loyal to it and to accept new products and innovations it offers."

Share of requirements. This measure requires some computation. First, define requirements. This is the total amount that the customer spends in the market space you are targeting. Most industries have a third-party data source for total market size, and some kind of panel data for expenditure by customer type. The pharmaceutical industry in the United States can track prescription units by drug type by doctor. The health care industry can track total health care spending by category by hospital or hospital group. In consumer goods, ACNielsen has a panel of households that track their total expenditures in a number of categories and this can be projected to the United States as a whole.

Second, measure your share of requirements. This is the expenditure of the customer or customer segment on your products or services in the categories or market spaces that make up the defined "requirements." These data can come from your internal sources or from a third-party measurement company.

Brand equity score. This is a survey-based metric, which we addressed in Chapter 5. You should measure three items:

1. Brand equity ownership (the one promise you want to stand for).

2. Category drivers (the elements of acceptance on which it is necessary for your brand to qualify to be considered by the customer, and on which it is necessary to win to be preferred by the customer).

3. General drivers of brand equity (such as differentiation, relevance, esteem, and knowledge).

Develop a score out of 100 for each one and add the three together to achieve a single brand equity score.

THE EXECUTIONAL DRIVER MEASURES

Innovation. There are two relevant measures of innovation: amount of innovation and quality of innovation. You will have to ascertain the right combination of quantity ("news") and quality ("breakthrough") over time. Quantity of innovation can be measured by the percentage of revenue your brand delivers via items or offerings that were not in the market in the previous period. You should benchmark this against competition (do you have more or less innovation revenue than competition?) and the category as a whole. You should also benchmark it against customer expectations, with a survey question such as "Which brand is the best at bringing you new ideas and solutions?"

Quality of innovation is measured strictly in terms of customer acceptance. This can be done at the premarket stage, trial stage, or loyalty stage. It should be measured in the premarket stage; a customer acceptance measure is usually defined as the score for "definitely or probably would buy." These are often referred to as "top two box scores" and should total 75 percent for a product that will be successful in the marketplace. The right innovation metric would be the number of concepts in the pipeline with top two box scores of 75 percent or more.

At the in-market stage, the measure is the customer acceptance of the new product or service, which is composed of trial (what percentage of target customers tried the new offering) and satisfaction after usage (either reported satisfaction or intent to repurchase).

Communication. Measures of communication should focus on success in getting the brand message across to customers. (The long-term effect of the message is captured in the brand equity score.) The typical measures are recall, persuasion, and wear out. Recall (percentage of audience remembering the message) measures the impact of your messages. Persuasion (percentage of audience expressing the desired attitude) measures the effectiveness in achieving the goal of attitude change or reinforcement. And wear out measures the decay in recall and persuasion that occurs with overexposure or excessive repetition.

For specialized elements of the communications plan such as direct mail, promotion, PR, e-marketing, and others, it may be necessary to devise tailored measures. However, the overall metrics of recall (was the message received), persuasion (was the message effective), and wear out (is the message still welcome) continue to be primary. For some promotion activities, you may wish to measure action—such as click through for web-delivered offers, or redemption for coupons and rebates, or attendance at sponsored events and trade shows. But, in the end, these are intermediate measures. What you truly aim for in communications is recall, persuasion, and continued openness to the message.

Brand touch. Brand equity is built via everything the customer sees, hears, and experiences. Brand touch is the experiential component. It includes the touches in the store or other retail outlet or office (such as the bank branch or the Federal Express office or Kinko's to which a user goes to drop off a package for delivery), at the call center, or on the Web. It includes packaging, merchandising, and sampling (such as encountering a cosmetics representative in the store, salon, or in the home or workplace if it's Mary Kay or Avon brand). It includes the direct sales call and presentation in business-to-business, and doctor's office "detailing" visits in the pharmaceuticals industry. And it includes the product or service in use. All of these brand touches can add to or subtract from a customer's perception of brand equity, and build or destroy the customer's affective commitment. It is important to measure these elements of brand touch and to create an overall measure of whether your brand touch contributes a positive or negative influence on brand equity and financial outcomes. The right measure is an experiential one: a survey question that asks whether the recipient of the brand touch took away a positive or negative feeling.

PULLING IT ALL TOGETHER: THE BRAND EQUITY MONITOR

This metrics framework can be viewed in its totality in a brand equity monitor, as depicted in Figure 9.4. This can be a digital dashboard or a scorecard presented on paper. It is composed of the financial outcomes, the brand commitment profile, the brand equity score, and the executional driver measures, all on one screen or one sheet of paper. The monitor should be reviewed by senior management with the appropriate periodicity—at minimum yearly, and ideally quarterly. Make sure that the measurements you put in place have the opportunity for meaningful reporting in those time periods.

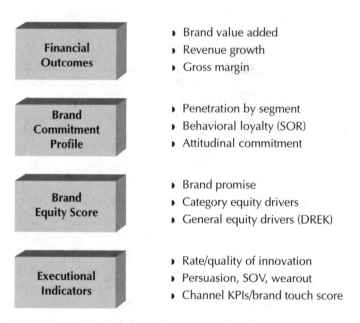

Financial Outcomes
- Brand value added
- Revenue growth
- Gross margin

Brand Commitment Profile
- Penetration by segment
- Behavioral loyalty (SOR)
- Attitudinal commitment

Brand Equity Score
- Brand promise
- Category equity drivers
- General equity drivers (DREK)

Executional Indicators
- Rate/quality of innovation
- Persuasion, SOV, wearout
- Channel KPIs/brand touch score

FIGURE 9.4 The brand equity monitor.

TOP DOWN, NOT BOTTOM UP

In the framework we propose, the viewpoint starts at the top—top-line revenue growth and gross margin at the brand level. It then works downward to shed light on each sequential driver: the brand commitment profile drives financial outcomes; brand equity scores drive brand commitment; and the executional drivers of innovation, communication, and brand touch drive brand equity scores.

Too often, marketing metrics have been approached from the bottom up, by focusing on the ROI of an individual activity such as an advertising or direct mail campaign, promotion, or trade show. In many cases, this happens simply because the measurement is easy: managers of direct mail campaigns are able to measure percentage response rates, and trade show promoters are able to measure traffic and attendance. However, starting from the bottom only creates problems. First, the measures are usually irrelevant. The response rate to an individual direct mail campaign is not a useful datum. Nor is the number of people who walked by your trade show booth. What is useful is whether brand equity and brand commitment are increasing or decreasing, and one direct mail campaign or one trade show is not going to be a significant contributor to that measure.

However, please don't take this to mean that we discourage the use of individual measurements of ROI for individual activities. One of our marketing heroes, Jim Stengel of Procter & Gamble, has declared publicly that *every* element of marketing expenditure at P&G must have an ROI measure to justify it; we respect and applaud that discipline. However, it is often very difficult to get the level of granular data needed to exercise such discipline.

Therefore, as you work your way in metrics from the top down, your first stop should be trying to understand the relative effects of the big "buckets" of innovation, communications, and brand touch, and to allocate resources between them accordingly.

The next stop is market mix modeling at the initiative level (rather than evaluations of individual programs). Market mix modeling is analysis of which groups or types of activity are contributing most to brand equity and brand revenue growth.

Market mix modeling has emerged as a credible way of estimating the relative efficiency of the major marketing expenditure choices. This welcome advance in marketing science can direct you toward the long-term goal of an "optimized" marketing budget. It does not help you to make choices between individual programs (such as a product promotion), but it can guide you toward a definition of what is the optimum mix of activities (between promotion, advertising, price reductions, and PR, for example).

Market mix modeling is a product of regression analysis, often multivariate. That means it requires historical time series data of sufficient duration to determine a pattern of cause and effect, and sufficient density to be able to isolate the effect of different types of marketing activity. The modelers often call the output the "due to" effect—how much of a revenue increase was due to activity type A (such as advertising) versus activity type B (such as sales promotion). Given the availability of data, market mix modeling can be quite discriminatory into how far it can break down the relative influence of different marketing activity—often into 10 or more discrete types.

But by its nature, market mix modeling is backward-looking, approximate, and limited by available time series data. A more sensitive and potentially accurate way to model the optimum marketing mix is agent-based modeling. Because it is a simulation, agent-based modeling can accept many more kinds of data than a market mix model—including survey data, nonlinear data, and even expert opinion. It can also simulate outcomes that market mix modeling could never contemplate, such as the "buzz" of word-of-mouth that can often carry a new product to early success, or the effect of distribution on awareness. As we mention elsewhere, leading marketers in many industries are pioneering in building experience with this tool, and you should become knowledgeable about it quickly.

Only after market mix modeling or simulation is complete do we recommend the analysis of individual programs such as advertising campaigns, direct mail campaigns, and trade shows. For each one you must determine the notional metric (how will I be able to demonstrate that it met the overarching goal of brand equity building as well as the efficiency goal of ROI?) and then make sure the data gathering methodology is in place before the activity starts. It is extremely difficult, if not impossible, to isolate data from one activity versus another, so you must decide how you will tackle this problem. You might compare activity this year versus last year using the "all other things remaining equal" principle. Or you may be able to hold out one region or one time period that did not receive the activity. Have your methodology, data, and business case argument in hand before you launch the measurement.

At minimum, it is a sound philosophy to "measure everything." With this discipline, you can only get better over time.

EFFECTIVENESS SHOULD TAKE PRECEDENCE OVER EFFICIENCY

Top-line revenue growth and gross margin are measures of effectiveness. These are the outcomes for which marketers strive and against which the function and the investment should be measured. Not much good can happen in a company that doesn't have top-line revenue growth, and that's what marketers concentrate on.

The same is true for brand commitment (both attitudinal and behavioral). These are measures of the effectiveness of marketing in creating outcomes. Similarly with a growing brand equity score, quality and quantity of innovation, and brand touch. All are effectiveness measures.

What of all the talk of marketing ROI? Isn't that an efficiency measure? Well, yes it is. And it is important. We don't seek effectiveness at any cost, but at reasonable cost. Return on investment can be defined as the increase in top-line revenue achieved per dollar of marketing expenditure.

Our point is twofold. First, concentrate on effectiveness. Second, apply the principle of top down, not bottom up, to efficiency measures. Thus, the first efficiency measure is total increase in top-line revenue over baseline, divided by total cost of marketing. This simple "one number" approach normalizes the return on all expenditures across the enterprise landscape. By focusing on ROI, management can choose priorities among expenditures as diverse as a new manufacturing line, a new piece of CRM software, a new sales team at a key account, or an increment in allocation of dollars to the marketing function. It can be easily accepted as a "fair" guideline, because everyone intuitively understands how the ROI yardstick enhances the overall efficiency of the enterprise.

Another top-level efficiency measure utilizes the brand commitment profile and measures the cost of moving customers up the attitudinal commitment continuum divided by the resultant revenue and profit increase from moving them up the behavioral benefit continuum.

At the level of each of the major executional drivers, a similar ROI analysis can be performed.

- The revenue contribution of innovation divided by the cost of innovation.

- The revenue contribution of communication divided by the cost of communication.

▶ The revenue contribution of brand touch divided by the cost of brand touch.

In each case the revenue contribution to the total can be derived via market mix modeling.

Go beyond this level (i.e., "lower" in terms of granular detail) only when all the measures listed in this section are in place, and when you are confident that the energy you expend on the analytical effort will return an equal or higher benefit. You might call that an ROI on analytic effort.

SEALEY ON METRICS

To provide further insight from experience, we asked Dr. Peter Sealey to provide his perspective on metrics. Sealey is CEO and founder of Los Altos Group, Inc. Dr. Sealey also teaches at the Graduate School of Business at Stanford University and has had a distinguished marketing career as varied as the first Global Marketing Director at the Coca-Cola Company and President of Distribution and Marketing for Columbia Pictures. He discusses the reticence of management to use metrics in marketing, how metrics can be used to set marketing objectives in the movie industry, and the positive developments for integrating the marketing mix effort with new technologies that provide better measurements.

Interview: Peter Sealey, former President of Distribution and Marketing, Columbia Pictures

Joseph Schumpeter (1883–1950), the Nobel Prize winning economist stated, "We live in a perennial gale of creative self-destruction." In business, the conventional models are pre-empted by newer models that have superior performance and results. During the transition period, the most difficult job for the management team is to abandon the practices that made them great and understand there may be a superior technology or delivery system that challenges their model. It's a natural resistance. However, there is no permanence to a business model. For example, the movie studios should have taken over television in its early years. They ignored it because television "was not their business." The television networks in the late 1970s should have looked at what Ted Turner did with CNN and cable TV and understood that they needed to get into satellite cable television. People do not listen to Schumpeter's message because it is very difficult to make transforming change from the inside.

Let's take those companies that use television as the primary means to introduce new products. In the motion picture industry from 1982–1992, the cost of introducing movies went up 741%, while the consumer price index went up about 90% during that period. In 1985, I could use network television and introduce a movie for the next day to the core target audience of young adults 18–24 years old. I could also wait six to nine months to understand what I would do to introduce the movie internationally. The cost increases to do broad-based advertising have become so cost exorbitant, it almost prohibits making a profit on most studio-produced movies. You cannot reach that 18–24 audience anymore, particularly the males. You no longer have the leisure of rolling out the introduction around the world at your own pace. You have to do it close to the U.S. opening because of the piracy issue. So, why are the studios still doing movie introductions the same way? Because they don't know what else to do! So, you have a broken model that will prevent the economics of the motion picture industry to be viable at the rate at which media costs are escalating.

All you need to open a motion picture over a weekend is five million people to come to a movie on a Friday night. The marketing problem could be redefined as, "How do we identify ten million people, half of whom may compose that audience of five million to come to that movie on Friday night?" They are using the broadcast television media and wastefully spending to attract those five million people.

The Measurement Systems are Lagging Behind the Marketplace

Integrated marketing communications used to mean consistency of message and style across media: measured broadcast and print media, publicity, point of sale, events, retail, promotions, etc. "One sight, one sell, one sound" was the mantra. It was simple with limited media choices.

Now, integrated marketing spans such a plethora of complex media, some of which is so difficult to get metrics. How do you get metrics for guerrilla marketing? In the old media model it was simple, "What is your reach and frequency?" We have still not found a way to explain the new media. The system of accountability and measurement is lagging behind the reality of the marketplace. It is much more difficult to integrate these new media using the old metrics.

The New Paradigm for Marketing Accountability

Suppose someone is thinking about taking a Hawaiian vacation. He types in to Google "Hawaiian Vacation" and sees two premium page search results at the top and seven or eight paid ads on the side as well as the hyperlink to the Hawaiian Visitors' Bureau site. That individual has raised his hand and said, "I am thinking about taking a vacation in Hawaii." Suddenly that person is fixated on that screen, because there is now a wealth of information, some provided free and some paid for by advertising, for that consumer to choose from. Say there is an Avis ad promotion for a car for a week in Honolulu and that person can enter a code and book his car right then through a hyperlink to the Avis site.

Avis has paid Google for that position and by each inquiry. Contrast that to the lack of accountability in broadcast television advertising. Some product categories lend themselves more to this approach, such as travel, financial services, and automotive. In the purchase of autos, the primary means for product and competitive price information is the Internet.

Important Categories and New Technologies for Marketing Metrics

There are really two important categories for metrics: perception and behavior.

1. The perception of the product or service in the consumers' minds. This includes their awareness and image of the brand. The marketer has to manage that process of building and directing the brand image.

2. The behavior toward that product. Is it under consideration? Has it penetrated the household? What is the frequency of usage and share of the category? What is the usage consumption? In short, this includes all the interaction in physical dimensions with the product.

We have never had a bridge between perception and behavior that we can clearly understand. That gap will begin to be closed by two technologies: Ad Id from the Association of National Advertisers (ANA) and the American Advertising Agencies Association (4 A's) that codes each ad to follow to the consumer level. This will be able to be tracked by household as well as individual viewer in the household.

The other trace is RFID (Radio Frequency ID), which is a chip on the package (similar to bar coding) that will contain a wealth of information about the product itself. The technology electronically uses the bar code to provide much more information, and this will be able to get to the household level of who is using the product. The ethical drug industry will be using this. They really need to know where the product is and who is using it. The combination of Ad ID and RFID will build that bridge between perception (Ad ID) and behavior (RFID). This will track whether this person saw the commercial and did she buy the product: when, where, etc. That is the Holy Grail of accountability.

Wal-Mart is adopting this technology in a big way. They are requiring RFID at the pallet level. Watch Wal-Mart and Procter & Gamble in their adoption of these technology metrics. Bar coding from the 1980s became the DNA for supply chain management. RFID has the potential to do the same to identify all products electronically with a wealth of information.

Here is an example for how it could be used: RFID could help monitor compliance by a senior citizen in the taking of correct medicine dosage. This would be a major benefit for a drug company to assure maximum benefit to the consumer for the efficacy for the drug being prescribed from that company. This can reduce the adverse effects of senior citizens not taking their correct dosages and having to go to the hospital for serious procedures.

Imagine One-to-One Pricing

Who says everyone should be paying the same price or receiving the same discounts for products? With retail stores and traditional coupons, this was a given. However, supposing you register with the P&G family of products and P&G gives you a consistent loyalty bonus at the store level. So, with the electronic coding, products can be related to one another from a company and a different price for each customer could be charged for the same merchandise. Or GM could provide an e-mail delivered promotion to everyone who brings a four-year-old or older Ford car to Jiffy Lube, and offer a new GM car to test drive for a week. Technology is going to permit truly one-to-one marketing. Right now it is one size fits all. In the future it will be one size fits one.

Be Proactive to Test the New Technologies

Accept that we are in a transformational stage. It will take time for marketers to adapt the technology. The question is, do you want to be proactive or be forced to take it on later in a reactive mode? Can we recognize junctures and be willing to experiment? You have to continue to probe and find ways to do it better. For example, how can marketers learn to use advertising in a portable wireless environment? Find ways to bring messages into that environment. You can sit back and do nothing or learn and experiment. It may not go anywhere. But if you learn to use it first—and educate yourself— you can lead. In the 1950s Procter & Gamble created the soap opera on television by early experimentation with a new media, and transformed its own company in the process.

SUMMARY

Good management requires good metrics. A "metric" is a performance measure that top management should review. In the case of marketing, these are financial outcomes and their key determinants: brand commitment, brand equity, and their major drivers (innovation, communication, and brand touch). Upward movements in these numbers are the measures of the effectiveness of marketing.

The ultimate efficiency metric is ROI. However, its highest benefit is realized at the overall level (ROI on total marketing expenditures), and you should be sure to have that capability in place before moving to focus on the marketing mix level and, lastly, the individual activity level.

chapter **10**

TECHNOLOGY-ENABLED ENTERPRISE MARKETING MANAGEMENT

➤ *Can your marketing capability embrace technology comparable to your supply chain?*

➤ *What technology tools can aid your marketing managers and augment their ability to increase ROI?*

➤ *How can you design a marketing portal so that it will be useful, broadly accepted, and transform how marketing is performed?*

➤ *How can you increase the value of your brands through the application of technology?*

In this decade, all industries have measurably improved productivity in large degree because of the application of information technology and the Internet. Network technologies and distributed computing have spread the power of technology-enabled business processes to transform most parts of the organization. Implementing enterprise applications such as ERP systems has forced organizations to capture and standardize their operational processes and enabled massive increases in effectiveness and efficiency.

Yet, the marketing function at most organizations is still operating with little information technology to support it. This deficiency in the use of technology in marketing as compared with other functions is illustrated in Figure 10.1.

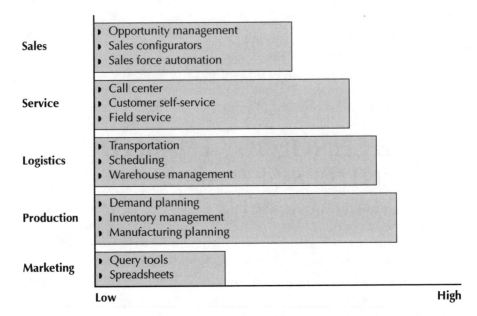

FIGURE 10.1 Use of technology by organizational function.

This situation is about to change dramatically. As marketers are held more accountable for return on marketing investments, they will be required to codify and standardize their processes in the same way as other functions. In the previous chapters, we described such an end-to-end process framework for building winning brands. The highest achievement of marketing will be to enable these processes with technology.

The challenge is to map the processes so they can be embedded in an organization and on the desktop of each marketer using IT applications and support infrastructure. Process mapping and enablement through IT is new to marketing, but it is not new to other functions. Organizations have implemented such efforts in other areas such as operations, finance, and supply chain. Hence, there is usually considerable organizational experience in designing and implementing enterprise applications. This learning can be easily transferred to marketing. While each organization has its unique experience, the following are important learning points common to enterprise application implementations:

Senior management sponsorship and alignment. Most enterprise applications subject the organization to a substantial upheaval and represent a period of disruptive change. Anything of this magnitude can succeed only if it has the visible and united sponsorship of senior management. Without sponsorship, such initiatives are likely to be rejected by personnel, most of whom are comfortable with the current paradigm. Industry statistics show that close to 30 percent of IT projects are canceled before they are completed and that over half have cost overruns. Slightly less than half have not delivered the business benefits expected of them. Many such projects fail from the lack of senior management attention.

The value of process. Many enterprise application implementations fail because the implementers are too focused on the technology rather than the business problems that they are trying to solve. Customer relationship management (CRM) was heralded as the solution to the silos across customer touch points. Many man-years of effort and millions of dollars later, the silos are still standing and CRM users complain that the technology is more a burden than a useful tool. Many such implementations are now categorized as "shelfware"—sitting on the proverbial shelf, without anyone using them.

Successful implementations require time and effort in determining and finalizing the appropriate business processes and rules before the translation into requirements for the technology. Treating technology as the starting point is often a temptation, and never the right answer.

Best practices content should drive process mapping. Process mapping teams in many organizations often produce mechanical, dry, long, and complex documentation. These documents are very impressive to present (as they can fill the walls of a large-sized room!), but are usually impractical, because they are too long and complex and lack good content that will accompany the process map. A process is manageable and implementable only when it is accompanied by the best practices content that guides the users of the process at every step. This content makes the difference in how easily the new process is adopted and how successfully it is implemented.

Pay attention to usability and user interface. Unfortunately, user interface and overall usability of a new application are often neglected. Business users are seen as captives, who have no choice but to use the application. Many good software applications are ignored in organizations because of poor usability. This is especially relevant to marketing applications, as the user base is very sensitive to graphic appeal. A user interface patched together by various software developers is usually undesirable.

Start small and grow fast, but build to scale. Many applications, especially in the marketing area, are developed as point solutions to address a specific pain point. This happened especially with the popularity of web applications in the late 1990s, where many rogue, independent department-funded projects were implemented to solve a particular issue in one area. These applications are often very difficult to maintain and upgrade although they may have very staunch support from their users. It is even more difficult to scale these applications to a larger user base and to expand functionality. At the same time, trying to "boil the ocean" by solving every issue simultaneously is not a very smart strategy either.

We recommend developing a modular architecture that can be modified over a period of time. This allows you to start small, but grow at the pace at which you are comfortable. Ensure that the design is scalable in size and scope to service the dynamic needs of the enterprise.

Involve people from across the organization. Rejecters of new application initiatives often state that because they were not involved in the design and development of the application, the proposed solution could not possibly meet their needs. Casting the net wide for input at an early stage is always a good practice.

Don't implement in silos. An important corollary to the point above is the scope of the project itself. Often, functional processes and applications are developed without cognizance of how these will interact with systems from other functions in other parts of the enterprise. A large global company that we have worked with has been developing functional capabilities in multiple areas such as supply chain, R&D, marketing, and more. Two years into this program they realized that while they are on target for improvements within each of these areas, they are still missing the bigger picture of integrating efforts across all parts of the enterprise.

Think early about adoption. Building an adoption program for your application should be actively considered and designed into the system early. Some companies identify critical parts of a process (such as getting approvals) and mandate that these can only be done within the new system. This forces adoption as well as delivering a benefit to adopters (faster, easier approvals).

Pilot. Executing a pilot is always a good idea, no matter how confident you might be of the developed system. The pilot always reveals practical difficulties in using the system, and quick fixes can be developed for these before the launch of the next release. More important, it provides a success story that can be replicated in other parts of the organization.

Invest in training. Companies often spend millions on a programming initiative and then cringe at spending a tenth of that amount on training. Both classroom and on-the-job training are useful in adoption. Training also helps achieve the business case faster by making the users productive early in the adoption phase. Identify a go-to resource within the organization beyond the initial training period. It is just smart business.

MARKETING IMPLEMENTATION

Marketing processes are very diverse in their scope and requirements. While strategic processes such as domain strategy and brand equity management usually involve a limited number of fairly senior managers, executing advertising, promotions, and event marketing involves a larger team, including personnel from agencies and vendors. You do not need to create separate applications, however, for each of these processes. The five most common categories of tasks that are used repeatedly in each of these processes are:

▶ *Program management*—defining, launching, and managing marketing programs and projects.

▶ *General collaboration*—enabling knowledge sharing and topical collaboration among teams outside the context of a project.

▶ *Marketing knowledge management*—collecting, sharing, and retaining marketing knowledge including consumer knowledge, success models, brand histories, and other assets for reference and reuse.

▶ *Marketing data management*—integrating data from internal company and external sources and providing analytical tools for processing that data.

▶ *Marketing planning*—developing, approving, and tracking plans, whether at an overall brand plan level or at an individual campaign level.

The tasks outlined in Table 10.1 are used throughout all the marketing processes.

TABLE 10.1 Marketing Process Tasks

Examples of:	Insights	Domain Strategy	Brand Equity Framework	Long-Term Equity Appreciation Plans	Annual Brand Planning	Implementing the Plan
Program Management	Managing the project of creating research plans	Managing domain definition and strategy projects	Managing brand equity definition and management projects	Managing the project of creating the 5-year LEAP	Managing the project of creating the 1-year annual brand plan	Managing the projects of creating and executing campaigns (e.g., advertising, promotions, etc.)
General Collaboration	Identifying and validating insight opportunities	Reaching out across the organization for data to help size the domain	Discussions among groups on how to update the brand equity framework	Discussing synergies across functions	Collecting competitive data to help update the brand plan	Polling users on potential ad concepts
Marketing Knowledge Management	Storing customer knowledge in the voice of the customer	Retaining knowledge of an organization's research into need states	Brand history and past success models	Previous year's plans	Previous year's plans and their performance review	Success models and past history of brand
Marketing Data Management	Customer data from various sources	Domain sizing data	Data on consumer needs and brand fit research	Customer behavioral loyalty data for scenario planning	Brand financials and market share data	Marketing mix effectiveness data
Marketing Planning	Research planning	Business planning	Rationale and input for LEAP	Brand equity planning	Annual brand planning and budgeting	Functional (e.g., media) and campaign (e.g., e-mail campaign) planning.

THE MARKETING PORTAL

The marketing portal brings together all these required functionalities to provide a consistent and smooth user experience. This usually involves the use of an enterprise portal solution that can seamlessly reach into many applications and present the data in a consistent user interface. The portal is the single access point to knowledge, data, best practices, and automated processes. *It is the technological realization of enterprise marketing management.* The marketing portal:

▸ Becomes the marketer's desktop. It brings all the data, tools, and information to marketers that they require to do their job.

▸ Is an enterprise software solution to support the end-to-end marketing process framework.

▸ Is highly configurable, to adapt its look and feel for the different divisions and brands within an organization.

How the marketing portal meets the functional requirements is described in the following.

1. Program Management

Marketers do most of their work in project teams. Whether it is a 24-month new product development project or a 6-week promotional project involving a free-standing insert (FSI) in Sunday newspapers, these projects have many similarities in the way they are defined, launched, managed, and closed. Marketers need a collaborative platform to plan, launch, manage, and track all their marketing programs such that all users have access to the project status and are able to easily share project files and information. This helps in managing highly complex marketing processes that involve participants from across functions and organizations. The broad requirements of marketers in this area include:

▸ Providing an easy guided path to completing the various steps required to create a project.

▸ Accessing best-practice-based, corporate-prescribed, ready-made projects with steps for the creation, review, distribution, and tracking of typical projects.

▸ Sharing a common platform among all participants for tracking the project activities and progress.

- Accessing contextually relevant best practices for doing each task of the project.
- Using an automated approvals system for delivering approval requests and tracking all approvals in one place.
- Tracking the history of events in a project for later analysis.
- Collaborating effectively and efficiently with other team members without having to sit through long status update meetings.
- Archiving closed projects in a common archive from which they can be retrieved to and modified for further reuse.

The technology tools that best meet these requirements are collaborative project management tools. It should be noted that generic workflow tools usually do not meet these requirements.

2. General Collaboration

Marketing processes usually involve people from various internal functions across an organization, and also agencies and vendors working together to produce the required deliverables. Technology can facilitate virtually all of this collaboration. The key requirements in this area are:

- File-based collaboration
  - Selectively sharing files in a central repository
  - Soliciting inputs
  - Maintaining version control
  - Searching for files within the repository
- Discussions across a geographically dispersed team
- Remote sharing of files in real time
- Project-related work is integrated with the e-mail system
- Key system tasks being performed offline
- Opinions being sought from within a certain group

General collaboration features like file sharing, document management systems, discussion boards, polling tools, and real-time meeting capabilities can meet these requirements.

3. Marketing Knowledge Management

We have identified in previous chapters that one of the biggest issues facing marketers is the lack of historical knowledge. Effective marketing requires easy access to knowledge of consumers, channels, competitors, and brand history. Such knowledge is invaluable in avoiding past mistakes and for reusing existing knowledge in various parts of the organization. Marketers are often frustrated by how difficult—if not impossible—it is for them to find the right information. The key requirements in this area are that it:

▶ Acts as a single repository for current knowledge and expertise: case studies, success models, consumer knowledge, processes, templates, checklists, models, project templates, examples, etc.

▶ Creates hierarchies of information based on taxonomy and offers a drill-down capability to users in one part of the information hierarchy.

▶ Provides categorization and search capabilities.

▶ Manages rich media assets.

▶ Stores and serves web-based calculators and other such tools.

▶ Sets access rights at the file level to provide access control.

▶ Determines linked files based on metadata similarity.

▶ Provides web-based access to users from across all parts of the organization.

Management-based knowledge management software tools are usually able to meet these requirements. Handling rich media assets, however, usually requires the use of digital asset management solutions.

4. Marketing Data Management

Marketers need data from disparate internal and external sources and a set of analytical tools to make fact-based decisions. The key requirements in this area are:

▶ Integration capability to interface with different types of data sources.

- Data extraction from relevant data sources, both external (e.g., syndicated data, advertising tracking studies) and internal (e.g., ERP, CRM).

- Cleaning and transforming data—normalizing, removing broken/incomplete records, etc.

- Loading data into a relational database in a data mart designed and optimized for marketing analysis, such as market mix modeling and scenarios-based planning.

- Marketing analytics
  - Market mix modeling and other causal modeling
  - Forecasting and time-series modeling
  - Agent-based modeling and other simulations
  - Brand equity monitoring

- Data management capabilities, including availability of
  - Standard queries
  - OLAP type capability to slice and dice the data
  - Report generation capability

- Dashboard capability to draw and analyze data and present it in the form of key metrics to managers with multiple-level drill-down capability in increasing levels of detail.

The typical IT tools required to meet these requirements are an ETL tool (for extraction, transformation, and loading), a reporting engine, dashboarding capabilities, and an analytical engine that allows both time-series and causal modeling.

5. Marketing Planning

Marketers need a tool to budget and plan their various programs from new product development and annual plans to advertising, promotion, and media initiatives. The capabilities required in this area include:

- Collaborative campaign planning.
- Best practice guidance on setting objectives.
- Modeling capability to support objective setting such as reach/frequency objectives for media campaigns.

▶ Preparing detailed budgets, using flowcharting tools for some campaign types.

▶ Integration capability to interface with back-end financial system for budgeting.

▶ Forecasting plan results on the basis of historical data and time-series modeling.

▶ Forecasting planning costs on the basis of historical costs and latest market dynamics.

▶ Approving plans through a workflow process.

▶ Tracking the plan performance and reporting.

▶ Closed-loop financing.

▶ Archiving of plans for reuse.

A campaign management tool, which includes campaign and initiative planning and campaign management capabilities, could meet the requirements highlighted above.

A PORTAL EXAMPLE

These are the five components of the marketing portal and the technology solutions that are usually available to meet these requirements. Kimberly-Clark (KC)'s Brand Builder is an excellent example of the enterprise marketing management portal. Jane Boulware, former VP Marketing Services at KC, describes below the usefulness of the portal:

> "Brand Builder was born of a need to support and build KC brands, specifically global megabrands that are key to KC future top-line revenue growth.
>
> Rather than attack or optimize (yet again) one portion of the marketing mix (such as media or packaging), KC is one of the few companies that recognized the need to address the whole of marketing, from insights generation to market execution and post analysis. KC's enterprise marketing management vision reflects the entire marketing process in an integrated, end-to-end way, beginning with world-class processes, adding training, and finally, enabling the processes and people with world-class enabling technology (i.e., the Brand

Builder itself). An integrated, end-to-end approach to marketing would not be possible without Brand Builder. Either making the link between strategy and data was too labor intensive and thereby incomplete or the linkages could not be made as tightly as we needed them to be so there was, in effect, no end-to-end capability. With the end-to-end process in place, marketing becomes an investment with an ROI, rather than merely a cost that required budget control."

SELECTING TECHNOLOGY VENDORS

Many technology vendors address several of the requirement areas we've described. While some are from general enterprise application vendors like SAP, others are from specialist MRM (marketing resource management) vendors like SmartPath and Aprimo. How do you pick the right technology vendor to help build the marketing portal? Here are some things to look for in a prospective technology vendor, besides the usual feature fit with their application:

- The vendor "gets" marketing and what you are trying to do. It is important for technology vendors to appreciate the breadth and depth of the marketing discipline in order for them to be qualified to develop the appropriate solution.

- Solid credentials in having implemented this kind of technology solution for other reputed clients.

- A scalable solution provider.

- Willingness to work with your business teams to adapt the solution per your requirements.

- Integration capability with the relevant applications in your enterprise architecture.

- A good and flexible user interface appropriate for marketers (not "techies").

- Stable financial condition.

SUMMARY

Enterprise marketing management combines process mapping, metrics, and technology to make the entire complex system of end-to-end marketing processes operational in the fast-paced, ever-changing workplace. This technology-enabled solution, when built with content and real work process purposefully integrated, in an easy-to-use interface, can enhance the creativity and leverage the productivity of every employee in the company. It can inspire people to innovate and to use technology to unleash creativity, increase effectiveness and efficiency, and fulfill people's desires to do great marketing to expand growth. That's the objective of the New Marketing Mission.

chapter 11

THE MARKETING KNOWLEDGE CENTER

> ➤ *Does everyone in your organization, in every country and on every brand and business, have access to the marketing knowledge and data he or she needs?*

> ➤ *How do you capture and share corporate knowledge within an organization?*

> ➤ *Can you accelerate the organizational and individual learning curve?*

SPEED OF LEARNING—A SUSTAINABLE COMPETITIVE ADVANTAGE

The marketing knowledge center (MKC) is the first step on the road to building a full-scale Marketing Portal, described in the previous chapter. The MKC provides the organization with an immediate competitive advantage: speed of learning. Studies suggest that the company that achieves first mover advantage gets about 60 percent of the share of a new market. Accelerating the speed at which knowledge and information is shared within an organization allows for the benefits of past learning to be applied and costly mistakes avoided.

The advantage also applies at the individual and team levels. The ability of a marketer to save time by understanding what has worked in other areas and why it has worked also gives that person the advantage in speed. This is significant because speed enables marketers to get through the routine tasks quickly and frees them and their teams to apply themselves to more creative, value added activities. In the mission to enhance the speed of learning within companies, the MKC contributes by taking marketers quickly up the learning curve.

Another advantage of the MKC is that the memory is shifted from individuals to the corporation. So you create a "corporate memory." You give your people the ability to learn on the job, get all key data quickly, and assimilate themselves in a new brand assignment very quickly.

WHAT IS A MARKETING KNOWLEDGE CENTER?

An MKC is a comprehensive corporate digital library containing all of the data necessary for your marketing department to function at peak efficiency and effectiveness. It's a collection of all your internal best practices and actions that you know have worked in the past.

An MKC embraces best practices in marketing processes, data, analytics, and modeling. It also includes best practices content (guides, tips, and templates) to assist in the tasks of marketing, tools to actually implement those marketing tasks, and metrics to monitor the effectiveness of marketing activity. Because the typical marketing knowledge center is deployed on a company's intranet, the data is available to all approved employees 24/7.

Creating an intuitively navigable MKC is the quickest and easiest way to begin your company's journey toward marketing excellence because it shifts knowledge from the erasable "write and rewrite" memory of an ever-changing human employee base to a permanent, growing, and synergistic corporate memory. Equally important, a marketing knowledge center is a continuously visible symbol to your marketing personnel that you are serious about optimizing their output.

WHAT IS THE BUSINESS PROBLEM WE ARE SOLVING?

Few companies have a comprehensive shared knowledge base for marketing. The need for this capability might lead to small bands of professionals planning to create their own electronic library for their brand, region, or functional area. The problem with such a narrow approach is obvious . . . no common standard across the company, no company-approved "best practices," no procedure for what's in or out, and no links to similar libraries outside the immediate area.

The practical results of this almost universal condition are as follows:

- Projects move slowly because a common process path does not exist.

- "The wheel" must be rediscovered, and mistakes repeated frequently, because corporate knowledge about what works and what does not has vanished with the relocation or resignation of a key employee.

- New initiatives fail or succeed randomly because no proven repeatable development process is captured in an MKC. Different divisions or brands follow different recipes for new product development.

- Investment dollars generate unreliable returns because what has worked in the past in a similar situation is lost to those new to the business.

- Human capital is squandered by needless searches, meetings, and debates.

WHAT IS THE VALUE OF AN MKC?

An MKC enables everyone in the company to share the company's best thinking about its brands and business. It makes best practices available so that employees new to the company or the brand can come up the learning curve rapidly. The MKC is even more important for global companies. Many regions outside the United States and Western Europe do not have good information and metrics. It provides easy access to the programs that have worked in other areas of the organization, and a common understanding about customers and competitors.

By creating a comprehensive, contemporary MKC, companies can raise the effectiveness levels of their marketing processes and marketing investments. This effectiveness dividend is manifested in several tangible ways. An MKC results in a greater percentage of successful initiatives, because marketers maintain a knowledge base of success models. A marketing knowledge center also raises speed and agility—including faster time to market—because marketers collaborate around known processes and knowledge. Everyone in the marketing department learns faster, and in the long term this creates a competitive advantage in speed to market.

A case in point is the $20 million shopper research initiative launched by Procter & Gamble in 2003. During a presentation at the Association of National Advertisers conference in August 2003, Jim Stengel, Global Marketing Officer at P&G, mentioned:

> "We (have) invested over $20 million to add to our consumer database including conducting a consumer study that was second in size only to the U.S. census. Our total consumer database includes more than 100 million consumers across 30 countries, 25 retailers, and 20 product categories. We are combining P&G's proprietary shopper research with retailers' intimate knowledge of their shoppers to help grow our collective understanding of our most loyal shoppers. We know that about 25 percent of our retailer shoppers represent about 75 percent of sales and profits. What you may not know is that the average retailers are capturing only one-third of the potential purchases even from the most loyal shoppers.
>
> In-store marketing has always been important to P&G. We have recently put a formal structure in place for gathering and sharing our internal knowledge on this topic around the world. We have created what we call a center of expertise dedicated to shopper marketing."

The research will be shared in an MKC throughout the company and everyone in the organization will know what they did not know previously. This is important because in-store communications or brand touch is a critical area for P&G. Using this data, P&G will now know more about a key area that affects their brand equities and the health of their business, as well as previously unknown facets of their customers' preferences. The company is poised to respond quickly to the requirements of their customers.

An MKC has certain other advantages that are less obvious but equally important. Specifically, an MKC:

- Encourages the sharing of success models between countries at similar levels of consumer or retail development. It can prove disproportionately valuable for global companies with businesses in data-poor environments such as China, Asia, Eastern Europe, Africa, or Latin America. Good practices established in one country or one geographic region, seldom transfer to others. The MKC can transcend these barriers. An idea for the same class of trade in South Africa may also work in Korea. Where marketers lack customer data, the MKC can produce world-class perspective.

- Provides a continuous teaching and training presence. Today, the average marketer stays in a position for less than three years. While training dollars have been slashed, the MKC becomes a reliable source of short-term knowledge about the current business as well as the long-term collective wisdom of the company's best practices. The MKC is a repository of learning. It serves as a continuous training device.

- Identifies a clearer idea of what the company does not know. Too often, the corporation doesn't know what it doesn't know, and even more dangerously, thinks it knows things it doesn't. This is especially true today, since headcount reductions have often eliminated expert departments and individual "gurus," who held the organizational memory in their heads. It isn't until a company has arrayed its data in a logical format and studied it that marketers realize more clearly and urgently what they don't know.

In short, an MKC is your company's customized marketing library. The center can be designed, constructed, and launched in a short period of time. It can run on existing technology and be made accessible from every marketer's desktop, as shown in Figures 11.1 and 11.2 on the following two pages.

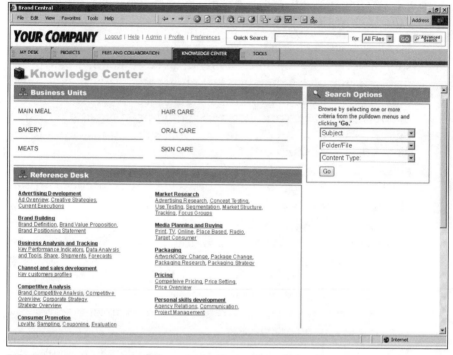

FIGURE 11.1   A conceptual view of a Marketing Knowledge Center.

A knowledge center home page on every marketer's desktop

Customizable by SBU, brand, or any other unit

Organized by knowledge type, or by brand, project, or any other method of choice

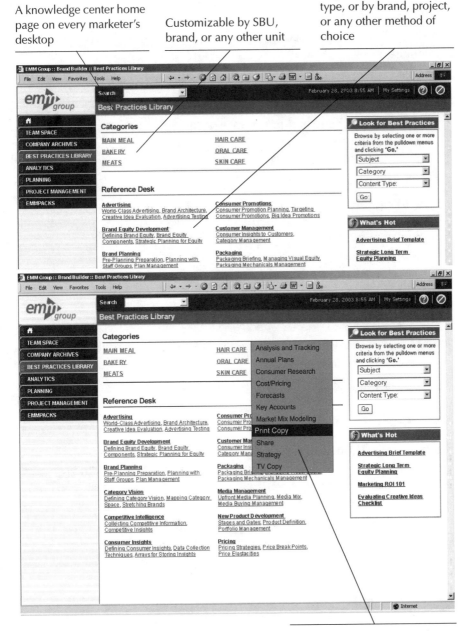

Pull-down menus help marketers find what they need

FIGURE 11.2 Another view of the MKC.

What Types of Data Should You Put in Your Marketing Knowledge Center?

A "best practice" MKC contains several different types of data and functionality:

- Current and past marketing plans by brand, category, or region.
- Historical "gold documents" that represent the best company thinking on the broad panorama of marketing issues.
- Approved marketing processes such as building brand equity, creating an annual plan, developing a media plan, and creating a major marketing event.
- Current and historical data on key subprocesses such as advertising executions, media spending plans by day part, promotional response by promotion type, distribution channel data, and key account plans.
- Important marketing articles from external experts.
- Chat rooms to "ask the company expert."
- Access to marketing Internet sites external to the company.
- Access to third-party marketing partners such as advertising agencies or media agencies.
- Samples of package designs and printed promotional materials.

How Does One Build a Marketing Knowledge Center?

- **Create a team.** Building an MKC requires multifunctional skills from the marketing function, from marketing research, from the IT department, and from external marketing partners who may contribute data or use the system.
- **Review the capabilities and requirements of your corporate intranet to ascertain its functional limits.** Important concerns relate to capacity, search and retrieval speeds, document-management capabilities, UI flexibility, and scalability.
- **Decide on the desired functionality.** A contemporary MKC will have certain basic functionalities including standard document-management characteristics, a keyword search function, metadata management, and access to external third-party marketing part-

ner resources. An MKC may also have a chat room functionality that permits members of the marketing department to access recognized corporate experts or third-party experts on a regular basis for discussions of issues.

▶ **Create a taxonomy.** Taxonomy is the way in which data is organized, such as the Dewey decimal system in a conventional library. There is no one right or wrong taxonomy. Because each company is different, one would normally expect data to be organized somewhat differently from company to company.

The most important taxonomic principles relate to the top levels of the organizing pyramid; does one organize around categories or brands or processes or geographies? Generally speaking, marketers prefer to organize around categories or brands at the highest level and then, beneath that, array data around specific tasks such as advertising development, media plan development, promotion, and so on.

This organizing approach allows a relative neophyte to go quickly to a document in a specific category for a specific brand for a specific issue.

Shown below is a typical simplified high-level organizing taxonomy for a marketing department.

Category or Brand
- Advertising
- Brand equity
- Competition
- Customer insights/research
- Marcomm
- Marketing plans
- Media planning
- Packaging
- Pricing
- Promotion
- Channel marketing
- Training

Each of the major sections above would have 5 to 10 subsections.

SUMMARY

By constructing an MKC, management takes the first step toward turning their marketing department into a "center of marketing excellence." The MKC will establish the basis for information dissemination, knowledge sharing, teaching, training, and motivation that can turn the current employees into an army of marketing experts who are agile, productive, and use company scale to advantage.

APPENDIX:
OPERATIONALIZING THE MARKETING KNOWLEDGE CENTER

▶ **Organize and commence document gathering.** Once you understand the way you wish to organize your MKC and the documents you need, you are ready to organize the gathering process within the company. To expedite the collection process, you need to match document types with their likely organizational owner and provide these owners with a simple format for returning the document to the central document "parking lot." This entire process can usually be done by e-mail that is returned with the appropriate documents attached. The collection format should facilitate the subsequent process of "meta-tagging" the document for inclusion into the application.

These requests for specific documents often engender anguish from the recipients, who will complain of the time it will take them to find it. The magnitude of the wailing is the surest proof of the value of the MKC—if the logical owner of the key document cannot easily find it, imagine how hard it is for the typical inexperienced marketer to access it. Now multiply the time it takes dozens of inexperienced marketers across the company to find dozens of unfamiliar documents in a typical year and you can begin to understand the value of a comprehensive MKC.

▶ **Load the documents and conduct an initial sufficiency check.** Follow the appropriate tagging mechanism to array the documents in the application. Conduct an initial sufficiency check. Which areas of the MKC have a range of documents you consider comprehensive? Which areas are light on or even totally devoid of any documents? Launch a second request for the desired documents. Widen the target for the missing documents. Share the final results with team members and a small group of prospective users.

▶ **Identify the key missing documents or data.** Rank order the missing documents or data by value to the organization. Develop a plan to find or create the information. Share the plan widely in the department and with outside parties.

▶ **Train the personnel on using the MKC.** Like any new tool, an MKC requires training. In the short term, MKC usage needs to be promoted in house, by e-mail campaigns, for example. One of the most important reasons to promote the MKC is to encourage submissions of new material. The better the material in the MKC, the more the MKC is used.

Operational Issues

Once an MKC is up and operating, your company will face several operating issues. The most important are as follows:

▶ **Content control.** Someone or some committee must control what documents merit inclusion in the MKC and what documents don't. Someone must develop the policies that control when a document is removed from the MKC.

▶ **Security.** Most companies feel uncomfortable permitting unfettered access to the MKC by everyone in the company. An MKC must have the capability to safeguard sensitive material through a system of password-enforced targeted access. One MKC of which we are aware had upwards of 60 different security levels. This is probably excessive but it is not unusual to limit sensitive data like costs, profits, new product development, and major promotional plans to specific "need to know" groups.

▶ **Maintenance resources required.** An MKC does not run itself. Someone must be trained and assigned to load material, remove material, respond to problems, evaluate user satisfaction, and bring issues to the attention of the policy control board.

chapter 12

TRAINING: THE FASTEST WAY TO GAIN COMPETITIVE ADVANTAGE

➤ *Do you have a marketing training program?*

➤ *If so, are you teaching best practice brand building?*

➤ *If not, what should you include in your program?*

➤ *Where can you go for best practice help in brand-building training?*

Everyone agrees that training is essential to the success of an enterprise. In the economics of learning, training is one of the knowledge transfer and assimilation tools with the highest return for shareholder value creation. Yet, few companies actually budget adequate time and funds to provide marketing professionals with the training necessary to be proficient. Fewer still have the comprehensive approach to marketing that links process, metrics, and technology to the growth of brand equity that we advocate in this book.

Some of the reasons for the lack of complete marketing training have been mentioned earlier but they bear repeating. These reasons include:

▶ The conviction that marketing is an art, not a process. Almost by definition, art is difficult to codify and teach. As the myth would have it, marketing is the province of the gifted artist, not the trained craftsman and therefore training is pointless. People are either creatively gifted or they are not.

- The misperception that marketing is a set of unrelated skills or crafts such as plumbing or carpentry or masonry. That explains why some companies conduct individual classes for "brand positioning" or "promotion development" or "media planning" and feel they have provided "marketing training."

- The failure of marketing leadership to capture best practices or "what has worked" down through the years, with the result that no material exists to share in a training course or identify as "Our Company's Way of Brand Building."

- Last and most important, the lack of an end-to-end process that is sufficiently codified that it can be taught as a coherent body of knowledge.

In this environment, it's no wonder that when times get tough, one of the first line items to get cut is marketing training. Over the past few years in company after company, marketing training has been reduced to the point of embarrassing inadequacy. (Imagine what would happen to a football coach of a losing team whose response to losing was to stop practicing.)

A welcome contrast is offered by Gillette's new leadership team. When Jim Kilts took over as the CEO at Gillette, he publicly *apologized* to the employees because their training had been so sadly neglected. Within his first year, he had mandated 40 hours of training for every marketer and provided the resources to deliver it.

But the Gillette company led by Jim Kilts is the exception, not the rule. Over 95 percent of U.S. companies have no coherent marketing training program worthy of the name. Astoundingly, 98 percent of advertising agencies have virtually no internal formal training.

That's why the largest marketing trade organization in the United States, the Association of National Advertisers (ANA), has stepped forward to fill the void by embracing marketing training as one of its five most important responsibilities to the marketing community.

The ANA knew the marketing community needed a comprehensive solution.

Figure 12.1 illustrates how ANA is leading the movement from the haphazard approach of training today to implementing a disciplined approach using the principles and practices we have proposed in this book.

From		To
▸ Ad hoc siloed processes		▸ End-to-end integrated processes
▸ Undefined best practices		▸ Corporate best practices identified—every step of the process
▸ Poorly defined metrics		▸ Rigorous metrics around every marketing decision
▸ No comprehensive infrastructure for marketing		▸ An enterprise-wide platform
▸ No tool-enabled marketing knowledge center		▸ Easy access to data through a common portal
▸ Poor data analytical capabilities		▸ Technology-enabled models
▸ Little or no training		▸ Institutionalized training program for all levels of marketers
▸ Silos of unshared marketing knowledge		▸ A collaborative culture of sharing
▸ Functional-centric organizational structure		▸ Brand-centric organizational culture

FIGURE 12.1   Brand owners need a comprehensive solution.

When the ANA's training evaluators saw EMM Group's comprehensive, end-to-end marketing process, they encouraged a collaboration that manifested itself as the Center for Marketing Excellence (CME). The CME was commissioned to create a series of consistent programs that has now been adopted by the ANA as the industry standard for training for marketing professionals. Most of what we teach in CME has been covered in this book, with additional materials available to you on the CME's website (*www.centerformarketingexcellence.com*).

The purpose of the CME program is to:

1. Power your company's growth via training in a set of tightly linked processes designed to build strong brands.

2. Provide training in a state-of-the-art marketing management system developed in leading marketing organizations.

3. Enhance the skills of marketers with:
   a. A set of courses that support each process.
   b. Real-life examples of the processes in action.
   c. Tools to support the processes.

Our approach is to construct training that integrates process, metrics, and technology to unleash growth via brand building. Accordingly, we believe there are four conceptual cornerstones to a marketing training program:

Processes. We believe in teaching an end-to-end process that starts with customer insights. Unlike conventional marketing training courses, we believe it is of primary importance to link the subprocesses such as annual brand planning or media planning to the overall objective of brand building, and thereby enhance the students' understanding of each component of the marketing value chain.

Metrics. Marketers should be trained in the value of metrics as a measure of "cost inputs to value output" ratios. These metrics must be embedded throughout the overall marketing process. Marketers must learn the language of the CFO.

Best-practices content. Metrics consistently confirm that the processes produce better results when marketers use proven best practice approaches at every link in the value chain. CME has captured and teaches those best practices in the ANA-approved courses.

Technology. Within most companies, the marketing department is the department least served by technology, apparently because it is a knowledge management discipline and not a transactional discipline. Advances in technology and some new tools showcased in the CME course now make it possible for marketers to learn how to bring new effectiveness and efficiency to marketing knowledge management.

Jim Speros, Chief Marketing Officer for the U.S. practice at the Ernst & Young accounting firm is the past chairman of the board of the ANA. He shares his thoughts on the role of training for marketing professionals and how the EMM Group/CME program can be utilized by companies to augment their own training programs.

Interview: Jim Speros, CMO, Ernst & Young

Somewhere between 10 and 15 percent of an employee's time should be devoted to training. This can be a combination of on-the-job training with formal courses. Lateral moves into other groups and mentoring programs are also useful. I require that every person in my Ernst & Young group take at least three training courses a year. Professional services such as doctors, lawyers, and accountants have certain ongoing education requirements to keep their credentials. That has not been true of marketing.

The way we quantify the return on investment in training is through client satisfaction surveys. The metrics we use are the level of satisfaction for the quality of the work, responsiveness, professionalism, and other qualitative measures. Did the work itself make a difference in the business?

Obstacles for Management Commitment to Training

If management is only focused on driving day-to-day sales and not on development of their people, then training will never be a priority. Management cannot just say that training is a priority, but they must also budget for it and allow their people the time to get away from operations to take training. They should also demonstrate through their own example that they themselves are willing to learn new things.

EMM Group/CME: A Positive Step for the Marketing Industry

The CME treats marketing like other professional disciplines such as law or accounting. It has a rigorous methodology with core requirements that people should take and then provides certification to those who have taken them. A lot of marketing training happens informally. CME codifies what all marketing professionals should know and provides great value to the industry.

A big role that the ANA fulfills is promulgating best practices. Training and enhancing the professionalism of marketing people throughout the United States is something to which we have to have a serious commitment.

CME can provide a foundation of core skill sets that every marketing professional should have. There are always going to be things that are unique to every company and industry that have to be added on. The main benefit of EMM Group's program is that it provides a core foundation—and then each company can build off of it. For example, managing an advertising agency is a core skill that every marketer can benefit from.

The company can then focus on its own unique industry and practices; thereby optimizing its effectiveness in training by combining the CME program with its own.

BUILDING BLOCKS TO AN EFFECTIVE TRAINING PROGRAM

Once marketers have taken the foundational CME courses, a marketing knowledge center, or a "brand-building center" as we like to call it, provides a source of continuous improvement as the repository for your company's marketing knowledge and ongoing training content. The combination of the CME courses and the marketing know-how in your company-specific brand-building center can be the quickest path to better marketing results and continuous improvement through training.

These are the building blocks to lay the foundation for organizational and individual training. Here are our enhancements to those building blocks:

ADVANCING FROM KNOWLEDGE TO TRAINING

A major advance in marketing effectiveness occurs when the MKC is programmed for built-in training. At least three levels of training are available:

On-the-job training. The more marketers utilize the MKC as the first stop for all of their project work, the more embedded the training capability becomes. Whenever a user searches for information or starts a project, the MKC can be configured to push appropriate knowledge for immediate use on the job. Research indicates that training is most powerful when it is delivered closest in time to its subsequent application, and that on-the-job training is far preferred by recipients to classroom training. The just-in-time approach we advocate results in a marketing workforce that is continuously upgrading its skills.

Self-administered training. To allow marketing users to catch up on all the latest knowledge and techniques, topical information can be embedded in folders and users can be tested on their knowledge. The company can monitor whether the user has opened the folder, read the materials, and answered the "test" questions. Marketers can acquire certification for every level from "boot camp" to "master class."

Seminar training. Given the appropriate network infrastructure, seminars on every topic in the marketing knowledge center can be video streamed to the desktop, and coordinated with PowerPoint slides and searchable text. The leading subject matter experts from within the company and outside it can be captured on video, and their knowledge and expertise streamed to every desktop on demand. Imagine the leading expert on advertising development and the use of quantitative advertising testing giving a free training session to new assistant marketing managers on demand, prior to their first meeting with an advertising agency. Perhaps a customer insights expert can instruct every researcher, R&D employee, and factory manager worldwide. Marketing training can be completed without expensive, time-consuming classroom learning and offsite gatherings.

Companies realize immediate results as well as longer-term productivity goals with this form of process-related skill enhancement.

Jim Stengel, in addition to his role as Global Marketing Officer at P&G, is also the new chairman of the ANA. He discusses how these concepts have been integrated into the training for P&G, and have become part of the transformation of the organization. He also reflects on the importance of training for a global corporation and illustrates how P&G has implemented both a change in orientation and the use of holistic process for the marketing function.

Interview: Jim Stengel, Global Marketing Officer, P&G

Training Is Building Community as Well as Competencies

Training has become a huge value in the company. We deliver it online, with mentors, in classrooms, on the job, and in every format proven successful for us. When we were losing our way in the late 1990s we lost focus on that. One of the most visible things during our comeback is that training came back as a priority. Training not only builds skills, capabilities, and competencies, but it also builds community. It builds emotional attachment, loyalty, and inspires people. At the end of the day that may be more important than the actual competencies that we build.

We are conducting training in innovative ways. We bring people together for a week-long college, and during change points in their career. P&G brings external experts in to train. We offer training on-demand that is web-based, as well as seminars on special topics that are planned well in advance in all regions of the world. We bring in masters in the marketing world to teach our people. We record programs on CD-ROM disks and online, so they are widely disseminated.

P&G now takes a global community and connected approach to everything, whether the program is generated in Cincinnati, Kobe, or Chile. The training goes all the way to the top to CEO A.G. Lafley. We leverage technology to build knowledge networks. We also leverage technology to improve touch. I have a quarterly webcast that can reach every P&G marketer in the world; they can see me, hear me, and I can show videos and presentations. It is a new way to share and build a marketing community. We have a tremendous knowledge source that is Internet enabled; we have built workforce communities that are Internet enabled. The technology has helped us be more in touch.

The training experience can be more than just on-site or at your desktop. We took a team of P&G marketers to the Cannes Film Festival for the first time ever. That was an intense training week.

Training starts the day you walk in and it goes on forever. At the end of the day the most powerful coaching is one on one; that approach has been a hallmark of P&G throughout our history. The manager and direct report relationship is at the core of our belief system: transparency, openness, and honest coaching have gone through an honest revival within P&G in the past several years as well.

Because CME attracts the leading thinkers in marketing from corporations and academia, conducts original research, and contributes new ideas and intellectual property to its domain, young marketers and seasoned practitioners alike realize improvements in their understanding and skills.

As the world moves toward enterprise marketing management as a holistic, global, data-driven, technology-supported method of driving EPS and brand asset value, the marketers trained in the best-practice processes will win!

SUMMARY

Training is a strategic imperative for companies who want to integrate processes, metrics, and technology to unleash growth. Training should take place within this framework and management should budget the time and funds for marketing professionals to become proficient in their discipline. Training should be focused on both marketing competencies as well as building community within the company for best practices.

APPENDIX:
LIST OF COMPETENCIES FOR CONSIDERATION IN A MARKETING TRAINING PROGRAM

Knowledge and Understanding

Company and Business Unit Knowledge

Legal Understanding of Contracts and Commercial Trade

Regulatory Requirements

Business Strategy

Channel Understanding

Competition Understanding

Customer Insights

Products and Services Knowledge

Product Stewardship

Sector and Segment Understanding

Manufacturing Knowledge

Sales and Marketing Planning

Strategy Development

Forecasting

Inventory Planning

Managing Market Research

Value Proposition Development

Managing the Planning Process

Pricing

Brand Management

Channel Management

Sales Organization

Strategic Thinking

Category, Product, and Services Management

Sales and Marketing Implementation

Negotiation Skills

Direct Selling

Customer Relationship Management (CRM)

Portfolio Management

Territory Management

Key Account Planning

Marketing Communications

Consulting Skills

Telephone Selling

Contract Management

Customer Profitability

Credit Management

Range and Space Optimization

Supply Chain Management

Complaint Handling

Measuring Market Success

Customer Relationship Building

Customer Training

Sales and Marketing Behaviors

Customer-Service Orientation

Political Savvy

Retail Operations Specific

Retail Operations

Suggestive Selling

Understanding Retail Standards and Processes

Labor Management

Inventory Management

Cash Management

Site Merchandising

Format Development

Property Selection

Hygiene and Food Handling

Maintenance

Interpreting Retail Site Results

chapter **13**

WHAT SHOULD YOU DO ON MONDAY MORNING?

If you have a marketing leadership responsibility, the chances are you've already been challenged by your CEO and CFO to stimulate growth and do it with fewer resources. You cannot meet this challenge without transforming the way you go about marketing in your company. Transformation takes time and effort, but you must start somewhere. This chapter is about the first few steps that start the journey of 1,000 miles. It's about what you can do next Monday morning to address your CEO's concerns.

WHY IS THE CEO STANDING IN THE MARKETING DEPARTMENT'S DOOR?

The CEO has nowhere else to turn. In most companies, cost cutting drives have stripped all other processes bare; nothing else can be cut to fatten earnings. The only choice is to drive the top line, and that is the primary responsibility of the marketing function. Corporate management is now looking to the marketing department to demonstrate that marketing expenditures can drive the top line.

You can begin your journey toward transformation of the marketing function today by selecting one or more of these five steps. Choose the ones that solve your most immediate need.

FIVE STEPS TO MARKETING EFFECTIVENESS

1. Create a Marketing Knowledge Center

Gather all the marketing knowledge that you do have, put it in a reasonable taxonomy, find best practices from other locations, and post it on your intranet so that everyone in your company can at least share what's worked.

A marketing knowledge center (MKC) is different from a marketing portal. It's a component in a portal. It's a well-organized and easy-to-navigate collection of all your internal best practices—things that you know have worked. This is especially valuable in global companies, where many of the areas outside the United States and a few other developed countries do not have good information and good metrics. These data-poor developing markets can see some of the programs that have worked in other areas.

So, the MKC has your golden assets: a brand equity building model, a process for successful new product development, a process for developing great advertising, a process for building a promotion that works, and so forth. Along with the "goldies," you may also put in your "oldies": original and seminal strategy documents, historical brand share and sales, past advertising campaigns, historical point of view documents, market research, and the like. Place it all in one "virtual file cabinet" on your intranet, so that everyone in your company can have an easy reference point to what it is that you know, so that they do not have to waste time and lose productivity in rediscovering the wheel.

One of the great advantages of the MKC is that it becomes a continuous training device. This is important because few people stay in the same job for more than two or three years. When they move to a new assignment, little is left behind; there is no repository of learning. The MKC becomes the perpetual repository of learning. It saves everybody time and money.

We always advocate that an MKC include something that we call the Voice of the Customer (see Chapter 3 for details). It includes everything that the company knows about its customers, such as demographics, buying behavior, their perceptions of your brand, what matters to them from a functional perspective (this includes a hierarchy of values and of needs), and competitive information. This helps in two ways: First you can find everything you know in one place, and second, now you can begin to understand what you do NOT know.

2. Create Shared Processes

Focus on the major processes that create value, like building brand equity, annual brand planning, or value proposition development. Create the appropriate process maps and get everyone on the same page. Process is not constricting; process is your guard against chaos. In every other aspect of business, process development has played a major part in creating competitive advantage and leveraging the scalability of the enterprise.

Process problems impede the speed of marketing. First-mover advantage usually results in a marketer winning the major market share of that particular space. Most often, the brand that obtains that share also is rewarded with a higher profit margin. Focus on speed! You will get the higher share, and a higher margin. Even as the "me too" product copiers come along, by being the category leader who innovates and initiates, you will continue to grow revenue and margins: that's the "return" in your ROI.

3. Use Information Technology to Enable Marketing

Many people do not like to be "tied and bound" to process; they push back against it. For them, process impedes creativity. The sword stroke to cut this "Gordian knot" of resistance is to link processes with automation support. Our approach is to find ways to drive the processes using technology, so that everyone knows the steps involved and the steps are easy to follow. IT can capture the best practices and best processes and make them available on desktops throughout the company, so that everyone can be on the same page. The sophistication and ease of use of the technology has caught up to the critical need of best practice process development and dissemination.

Process and knowledge bundles can be captured in lightweight HTML software to run on any corporate enterprise platform, thereby eliminating the need for major investment in new software licenses.

4. Measure Outcomes in a Common Framework

The sharing of common metrics and evaluation procedures will accelerate the learning curve and enhance the effectiveness of individual and organizational performance.

A framework is a customized structure built to house information and data in practical, user-friendly formats. The framework can differ from industry to industry, but you need to select a framework to start.

The framework can be very simple. For example, marketing in virtually all businesses can be thought of as a trade-off between increasing penetration (new trial) versus increasing the share of sales to one of those customers who is already in your franchise (loyalty). The marketing imperative question is this: What is the best expenditure of your dollar? Should you focus more resources on attracting new customers or on getting a higher share of those customers that already exist? A simple framework can be built to measure which approach (or what mix of the two approaches) optimizes revenue growth and profitability.

Alternatively, the framework can be very sophisticated. You can divide your audience up into multiple segments and for each of those segments, ask: What percentage of my customers are in each of these segments? How much revenue do they generate? What is the total profit pool available and therefore, where should I be focusing my marketing efforts? Once you understand where you are focusing your marketing efforts, the inquiry moves to which marketing component will provide the greatest return against that particular segment of the audience.

Unfortunately, one of the inhibitors to action is that many marketers look for the perfect measurement. This is a classic case where "the perfect is the enemy of the good." Do not wait for perfection in measurement! Well-conceived but approximate measures are better than no measures at all.

5. Focus on Building Brand Equity

If you enhance your brand equity, your marketing ROI will go up. Once your brand equity starts to increase, you will find out that all your other marketing expenditures will also improve in their efficacy.

We believe very strongly that each brand must have a model to measure brand equity. The first step is to measure the degree to which customers associate your brand with that one word or one set of words that represent your message—the brand promise.

You need to measure and understand your advantage compared with your competition. Then you need a standard model to measure brand equity over a period of time. Process and technology enable continuous tracking and refining of brand equity measures. There are several of these industry-accepted models, and any advertising agency or consultancy (including EMM Group) can recommend one.

Shareholder value creation is directly related to your brand equity. The effectiveness of your marketing expenditures is tied to brand equity. Therefore, develop and build your brand equity model, and begin to measure how your individual marketing plans deliver enhanced brand equity.

SUMMARY

Successful marketing organizations must become converts to process engineering, meaningful metrics, and technology in order to claim accountability for increasing shareholder value. The marketing function must either transform itself or continue to hemorrhage corporate resources in wasteful, sloppy practices that would not be tolerated in any other function of the business. Management must take action.

Until now, management could claim it lacked a coherent vision of an effective future of marketing. With the publication of this book, we hope to provide the vision of the future, a pathway to guide you, and the mantra to inspire you . . . process, metrics, technology.

Now all that's missing is the will power and tenacity to turn vision into reality.

Remember: There's a little old lady in Des Moines who's your shareholder and she's depending on you.

Glossary of Acronyms

ANA	Association of National Advertisers
B2B	business-to-business
B2C	business-to-consumer
BAV	BrandAsset Valuator
BU	business unit
CEO	chief executive officer
CFO	chief financial officer
CIO	chief information officer
CME	Center for Marketing Excellence
CMO	chief marketing officer
COO	chief operating officer
CRM	customer relationship management
CXO	chief <area of responsibility> officer
EBITDA	earnings before interest, tax, depreciation, and amortization
EMM	enterprise marketing management
EPS	earnings per share
ERP	enterprise resource planning
EVA	economic value added
FSI	free-standing insert
GRP	gross rating point
IMS	integrated marketing strategy
IP	intellectual property
IT	information technology

IWIK	I wish I knew
LEAP	long-term equity appreciation plan
M&A	mergers and acquisitions
MCB	master creative brief
MKC	marketing knowledge center
MRM	marketing resource management
MT	marketer technologist
NOPAT	net operating profit after tax
OLAP	online analytical processing
P&L	profit and loss (statement)
PDA	personal digital assistant
PR	public relations
R&D	research and development
ROI	return on investment
ROMI	return on marketing investment
SOR	share of requirements
TCO	total cost of ownership
TRS	total returns to stockholders
VOC	voice of the customer

Glossary of Terms

ANA

The Association of National Advertisers. The leading marketing trade organization devoted to the propagation of Best Practices and the protection of marketing from legislative and regulatory evil.

ASP (Application Service Provider)

A software-enabled service that offers consumers goods and services over the Internet. Priceline is an ASP; Amazon.com is an ASP.

Best practice

The best way to perform a business process.

Brand activation

The execution of the marketing plan and marketing mix that connects the Brand to the customer. It includes Product Development, Advertising, Media Planning and Buying, Promotion, Direct Marketing, Interactive, Brand Touch, PR, and other such processes.

BAV (Brand Asset Valuator)

The trade name for a specific approach to measuring brand equity. This approach was developed by the Young & Rubicam advertising agency.

Brand building

A complete process for increasing the brand equity measure and the outcomes that proceed from it so as to achieve growth levels above category norms or above peer brands and companies.

Brand-centric

A type of marketing thinking that focuses on the ability of the brand to change attitudes and build brand equity, in the sure knowledge that these will change customer behavior.

Brand challenge

An assessment of the barriers and obstacles the brand must overcome to realize its vision, and the numbers it must achieve in its brand equity scores, penetration, loyalty, and financial outcomes.

Brand commitment profile The causal relationship between the number of target audience members who are located in attitudinal commitment segments (e.g., "aware," "accept," "adopt," "adore" attitudes to the brand), and behavioral commitment segments (e.g., non-users, low share of requirements, medium share of requirements, and high share of requirements).

Brand equity A measure of customer perception of the brand based on everything the customer sees, hears, and experiences about the brand. Brand equity is measured by survey data. Brand equity is a direct driver of financial outcomes, especially top-line revenue growth and brand gross margin.

Brand health A set of metrics that are displayed and integrated in a single statement or dashboard, which can be viewed as a monitor of a brand's well-being. Includes brand equity measures, financial outcomes reporting and competitive assessment.

Brand planning The brand's one-year business plan and budgets to meet its immediate financial targets as well as the long-term equity goals.

Brand promise The statement the brand makes to the customer delineating the need it will meet for them better than any other brand, and the emotional benefit they will experience as a result.

Brand touch The proactive management of everything the customer sees, feels, hears, and experiences about the brand when considering it, purchasing it, and using it.

Brand vision A structured statement of what the brand aspires to be in the future as a business and in terms of customer perception. Includes statements of customer targeting, domain strategy (the expanded need spaces where the brand will serve customers), positioning, and brand character.

Cash flow The net flow of money in and out of a business—the cash earned by commercial activities.

Category A narrowly defined set of like products, such as "the business desktop computer category." Usually defined by services that measure the volume in the category or the retailers and distributors who organize their businesses by category.

CMO

Chief Marketing Officer as an executive (rather than staff) position.

Configurable

Ability to make minor predictable changes to a software application that can be easily carried forward in a system upgrade.

Content

In the EMM Way of Brand Building we use the term "content" to mean those descriptions of best practice that help users execute the business process at the highest possible levels of effectiveness and efficiency.

CRM

Customer Relationship Management software and associated processes.

Cross Trend Analysis

An approach to developing insights by focusing on the implications of the interaction of two or more developing trends in the external environment.

C-Suite

The positions of CEO, CFO, COO, and some selected others such as Chief Counsel, considered as a group.

Customer loyalty

A behavioral measure of the customer's commitment to the brand based on the percentage of his total purchases in a category allocated to the brand over time (also referred to as Share of Requirements or SOR).

Differentiation

The customer's perception of the distinctiveness of the brand versus others, created by the communication and fulfillment of a unique brand promise.

Domain

A linked set of consumer needs that can be met by branded solutions. Examples include "confidence in reliable technology that's easy to buy, easy to use, and easy to own." Defined by customers based on their emotional and functional needs.

Effectiveness

The ability to favorably drive outcomes of revenue growth and gross margin improvement.

Efficiency

The ability to achieve effectiveness at reasonable cost (cost per unit of outcomes).

Enablers

Tools, guides and other aids to help users execute a process.

Enterprise Marketing Management	Managing the marketing process with world-class efficiency and effectiveness by every marketing practitioner across every brand enterprise-wide. The combination of process, metrics, and technology developed by the EMM Group.
ERP (Enterprise Resource Management)	The software-enabled approach of efficiently managing resources, especially raw materials, within a manufacturing process.
Esteem	The extent to which a brand commands respect of customers by keeping the promise it makes to them.
Ethnography	A research technique whereby researchers observe customers in the normal course of their daily activities; useful in creating observations and hypotheses for new insights.
EVA (Economic Value Added)	The amount of value created (usually defined as net operating profit after tax or NOPAT) over and above the cost of capital required to create it.
Gross rating point	1 gross rating point = one percent of a defined target audience reached one time by a communications vehicle such as a TV commercial.
Growth	An increase in the gross revenue generated by a corporation, business unit, or brand, usually in a one-year period.
Hierarchy of needs	The needs a customer seeks to meet via the use of a commercial solution, arranged in ascending order of importance. The highest level needs are emotional, such as the need for confidence or self-esteem.
HTML (Hypertext Markup Language)	A software language used to translate information into a format usable over the Internet.
Imperative	One of a small number (5–6) of major strategies which, if achieved over the five-year period of the LEAP, will result in the achievement of brand goals. Example: "achieve a brand equity score of 66% and a distance versus competition of 30 points for our new brand promise."

Initiative

One of a small number of specific undertakings in a brand's annual plan. An initiative may include multiple tactics, but is contained within a specific time frame, budget, and measurable set of objectives. Example: "increase penetration of target audience from 10% to 15% via a new product launch in the first quarter."

Insight

A profound understanding of the customer and the customer's needs that leads to a business idea that drives profitable growth.

Insights

This is a process for systematizing the conversion of the myriad of facts/observations into insights, the profound understanding that leads to a business idea that drives profitable growth. Insights are the lifeblood of a successful marketing program and drive the strategy, planning, and marketing execution of the brand.

Integrated marketing

A planning process that ensures that the right marketing vehicles are deployed in the right combination and at the right weights to achieve the marketing objective in an optimal manner.

Integration

The creation of a single solution using two or more software components. Data integration implies the combination of two or more data streams in one database.

IT (Information Technology)

Sometimes used as an all-encompassing group adjective for the technologies themselves (including hardware, software, and networks), and sometimes to refer to the corporate capability or department that designs, deploys, and maintains the corporate IT environment.

IWIK ("I wish I knew")

A specific activity within the EMM Way of Brand Building. IWIKs start the insights development process by their inclusion in Landscape reports.

Knowledge

The depth of customers' understanding and experience of the brand.

Landscapes

A document in the EMM Way of Brand Building. Landscapes provide each functional department with an orderly way to convey their functional experience and needs into an annual planning process.

LEAP	A five-year plan to set the long-term vision for the brand, with specific numeric targets.
M&A (Mergers and Acquisitions)	The business discipline of evaluating and facilitating the sale of assets from one company to another or the acquisition of company A by company B. M&A is what investment bankers do.
Marketing	Understanding the needs of consumers and meeting them through products and services. Marketing focuses on changing the attitudes of consumers and thereby driving buyer behavior.
Marketing Knowledge Center	A component of the Solution Stack that serves as a company library and reference source for existing marketing knowledge, best practices, and success models.
Marketing metrics	A comprehensive metrics structure that links a brand's financial outcomes to the strength of its brand equity. This, in turn is linked to each of the three executional drivers of innovation, communications, and brand touch.
Marketing mix	The combination of marketing tactics deployed to achieve a specific objective.
Marketing ROI	The profit from a marketing induced behavioral response divided by the cost of the marketing program to which the behavioral response is attributed.
Market mix modeling	An analytical discipline that seeks to establish the relative efficiency of various marketing spending choices (TV, magazines, e-Marketing, etc.).
Master Creative Brief	A document within the EMM Way of Brand Building aimed at aligning all of the brand's diverse messaging elements around a few core principles.
MRD—The Market Research Department	The functional experts within a company charged with the responsibility of understanding consumer behavior and attitudes.
Need space	A conceptual space on a domain map which describes a discrete customer need, such as a customer's need for reliable wireless communications via a laptop computer, which is a subsidiary need within "confidence in reliable technology that's easy to buy, own and use."

Process	A system for creating customer value that consists of activities or tasks, inputs to and outputs from each task, and measurements for the customer value of each output.
Product-centric	A type of marketing thinking that focuses on the ability of the product (or service) to deliver on functional performance measures in order to win sales.
Profit pool	The total amount of profit available to all brands operating in a specific market space. Each brand seeks to maximize its share of the profit pool.
Promotion	The provision to the customer or prospective customer of an incentive to purchase which supplements the value proposition of the regular offer.
Relevance	The ability of the brand to address the needs of a specific group of customers.
SAP	A German software company who pioneered enterprise resource planning software and other software-enabled approaches aimed at integrating activities and transactions in both the demand and supply chains.
Scenario tool	An approach to assessing implications of events or trends in a competitive marketplace.
Shareholder value	Number of shares outstanding multiplied by the price per share.
The Solution Stack	A solution architecture for the end-state vision of an enterprise system to support the end-to-end EMM Way of Brand Building.
Standards based	Standards-based software is developed on accepted industry standards (e.g., XML) rather than proprietary system standards.
Supply chain	The series of activities that occur after a customer places an order with a supplier and the supplier attempts to fulfill the order.
The Center for Marketing Excellence	An EMM Group subsidiary that collaborates with the ANA to deliver Best Practice training in a broad range of marketing areas.

The EMM Way of Brand Building

An interconnected end-to-end series of technologically enabled marketing processes and metrics which when taken together increase brand equity, consumer loyalty, brand sales, consumer satisfaction, and shareholder value.

The moment of truth

During the experiential chain of touch points between customer and product, a seminal event that affects attitudes or behavior in a decisive manner.

The Voice of the Customer (VOC)

A collection of critical facts and conclusions about customer behavior and attitudes toward a brand arrayed in an orderly manner which facilitates sharing among the company's marketers.

Top-line revenue

Revenue generated by completed sales, often known as sales revenue. This is a "top-line" number because it is usually the first line in a P&L or income statement.

Total Cost of Ownership (TCO)

The complete cost of defining, developing, testing, and maintaining a new IT solution. Includes all components of the cost including software, hardware, networking, and services.

Young and Rubicam

A marketing services company owned by WPP.